SUGGESTOLOGY

The Love of Learning

by

DR GEORGI LOZANOV as told to DR MEL GILL

First published in Chicago, Singapore and Bulgaria 2013
by Pandora Publishing House (Europe Division)
www.PandoraPublishing.com

All Inquiries, including Bulk Discounts should be addressed to
The Publisher :

Pandora Publishing House (USA Division)
205 East Butterfield Road, Suite 138
Elmhurst, IL 60126
Tel: (630) 908 2948 (Chicago) (914) 230 4933 (New York)
E-mail: enquiries@pandorapublishing.com

1. Thought and Thinking. 2. Psychology, Applied. I. Title.
153.42
The publisher and author expressly disclaim liability to any person
for the consequences of anything done or omitted to be done by such
person in reliance, whether in whole or in part upon any part of the
contents of this publication.

Contents

❧

Dedicated

To all those who love to learn
and learn through love.

CHAPTER 1

How quiet. How quiet the world was, just then.

The Viennese sky was grey yet again and showing no signs of improvement. A week's worth of the last warm rain of the year could be seen washing down the streets from the second floor view. It was September, mild and light as always in the dim of the late afternoon.

He was waiting for her downstairs. Today, they were to continue the interview about the latest development of their work. It would all be documented and preserved long after she was gone, of course. A standing legacy not only to her, but of their partnership together, and years' worth of blood, sweat and tears all for the sake of education. She smiled to hear the hectic opening and closing of the study door as he paced below.

"Eve, are you coming down? We have no time." The self confident voice held a weird, almost frantic note but was kind at the same time. Oh, how she wished she were more confident as she straightened her skirt for the third time, with unsteady hands smoothing away non-existent wrinkles.

It made her grey eyes sting and shine to consider just how right he was. They really did not have any time any more. Not after today.

"We have so much work to do!"

"My love, my dearest Georgi!" She whispered to the mirror, watching her as the meticulously applied eye color slid down her cheeks. Now, she would have to fix herself again. Redo everything so that he would not see that she had been upset and crying. She did not want him to worry for her. Not yet.

"He will never change. Oh," another sob shook her whole being as she washed her face. "How am I to tell him what the results are? Who will be taking care of him when I am no longer here?" She had spent most of the day like this, ever since returning from the doctor's office a few short hours earlier.

After receiving the news, there was not much left to do except weep. Weep and hope her love did not suffer too greatly after she was gone. There was still so much to be done. He did not have time to suffer.

Fixing her face once more, she looked herself over in the tall dressing mirror taking in her appearance carefully. In her mind's eye, she still saw herself as the 33-year old self she had been, preparing for a date with her lovely doctor, who now waited downstairs for her. Her reflection, however, showed another, older face that looked very tired. Too tired, in fact, for all the smiles she put on for everyone to see. Where were those smiles now, when her face was so pale and her eyes threatened to water all over again?

Where was that 33-year- old singer she had been? Gone! Gone on to better things, and bigger worlds than opera houses and solo productions.

Instead of that bright-eyed young woman, now she saw herself the way she truly was. At 59, dressed in her favorite cream-colored suit, and ready to face the world, she was a sight. Those who had been asked would say she had only become more beautiful with age.

Sometimes she thought she could see it as well, but it wasn't something to dwell on. Neither was this. No problem was solved by moping around. She logically knew that.

So why not straighten her shoulders and simply march down stairs, her inner voice asked? Because, her inner voice was not the one who had to the speaking.

Her inner voice would remain silent while a quivering soprano would stumble over the truth. Her inner voice did not have to tell *him*.

And, what of him? Was she ready to face her beloved? Was it to tell him that she would be going soon? She doubted anyone could ever be prepared for such a thing … especially for that, but it mattered not. He was waiting for her.

Down the carpeted staircase, echoing through the still air the potent voice of Boris Christov cut the calm of the neighborhood. Once again, his favorite "Na mnogaia leta" made the very floor tremble. It seemed one could not hear the throaty bass without stopping at least for a moment to listen in awe.

Repeatedly the sound thundered off the walls, through the windows and past the very ears to the mind itself. To penetrate the heart within and bring to a grinding halt the very individual. She would often find him just so, frozen in place over the typewriter; eyes closed as he drank in the powerful tone and when he would finally look up, she would see in his eyes… the longing. It picked at her open heart like a flock of scavenger birds, the sight of that longing in his face, that yearning for his Bulgaria.

One day, she knew he would return. They had planned to for several years and been talking about it off and on for a while now, but what now? Would it be this year? The thought curled her lips downward in a frown. She hoped not.

If they were to return, she hoped the reason would not be related to what she had to tell him today. Why not a better, happier reason? Why not *any* other reason than *this?*

Just the idea and she was ready to well up again and weep. Yes, weep for it all and feel sorry for herself. But no! The time had passed. Now it was time to do, instead of a dream of things that simply could not be.

"Eve, please, come and listen to him! What a voice!" Yes indeed, what a voice, though it was not the opera singer who made her smile just at the sound of him. "Are you ready? Where did we stop the last time?"

Oh, how much she loved his eagerness. Almost like a little child, he was animated in his enthusiasm. Such fiery spirit had almost cost him his life before they even met, and still he did not learn, and she was thankful for it. After all, where might she be today, had this strong, striking spirit been any less stubborn?

Very lonely, she imagined with an inward smile as she approached the study. Dark wood gleamed all around, polished from floor to ceiling and everywhere in between. Wall-to-wall bookshelves towered around the familiar study, making her heart twist at the sight of it.

They had not lived here very long and yet; she already regretted the fact that she at least would be leaving it soon. Too soon and if she had her way about it, she wouldn't leave but there was just no other way. Not unless she chose not to tell him; but how? How could she keep such a thing from her love, her partner?

Obviously, it wasn't even a question.

Softly, as though her voice would break the very air, she drew in a steadying breath and spoke. "Georgi…I have some news for you."

He stopped and looked at her. Startlingly green eyes, like the depth of a dark ocean they had often flown over peered at her over the top of his twinkling spectacles. She felt her heart flutter at the sight as it had so often through the years. It was nice to see something never did change.

"What is it, Eve? Have they phoned for the training? How many people are there already?" Shaking his head at her, the doctor smiled warmly. "We cannot take more than three. I have told you."

Yes, he had told her. He told her twice, then a third time just to be sure. She smiled for one fleeting nanosecond, little corners of her heart-shaped mouth flickering upwards for just a moment…then it was gone.

Her eyes were clear as she looked up at him. She even managed a real, honest smile at the tiny shaft of sunlight that filtered through the window to dandle his curly white hair in the curve of his shoulder. He loved to wear it long, and the sight of it had her hand reaching up to detangle a strand where it wound around his glasses.

"I have cancer." She said calmly and almost softly. There. She had said it.

Years of training her hands to play her beloved violin, her voice to sing grand arias, all the discipline…every moment she had thought might prepare a person for just this sort of thing had not readied her for announcing the news. Nothing could have; she realized somewhere in a little corner of her mind as she watched him carefully.

Somehow, after agonizing over it all day it just came naturally. Did Mimi say it much the same way to her Rodolfo? Were they that different from Puccini's lovers in La Boheme?

Cancer, her life was over, fluttered by on the wings of little lavender butterflies that came with the spring, and by summer were nothing more than fleeting memories.

Unlike those tiny little jewels of wing and dust, she would not return in the spring the next year. Her time was close. What work they had yet to do would be finished, of course.

There was time enough for that, but what of them? Was there really enough time for the one you love, once you realize you will have to leave them? That your time together will not be eternity? Of course, no one's time together would ever be *eternity,* but it was hard to understand that until time was up.

Until then, you always had plenty of time; time to waste, time to pick away at the moments of the dull day. Time to rush and fly with frenzy over whatever life-changing catastrophe was going to kill you at just that moment. So much *time* and now … it was all gone.

For a long, lingering moment, he simply looked at her. At first, she almost wondered if she hadn't spoken at all. It felt as though the world would collapse under the pressure as she waited for him to say something … anything.

Then, all at once, she watched his shoulders fall and deflate as though suddenly, he alone carried the burden of Atlas. Taking off his glasses, he sank into a nearby chair. Papers, bank letters and a book or two slid from the desk into a heap on the floor. He didn't notice. He didn't seem to care.

"Eve!" His voice was part question, part prayer. From the bedroom, the voice of Boris Christov filled the silence solemnly singing "Zhertva Vechernaia" as he gathered himself and the tools of his formidable intellect to overcome this new challenge.

"They are wrong." He shook his head adamantly. "The results are wrong."

"They are not wrong, Georgi." Somehow, now that the news had been revealed, she was feeling better. Her brilliant love could not say the same. She could see it in his face, in his eyes, the worry. He would now worry and argue against it until he was proven wrong. Such was her love. But oh, time was so short. What was the point in crying over it? Now, especially now that every second was so very precious.

They still had so much to do. She could see him, watching her with those stubborn green eyes. He was looking at her radiant beauty, her small hands, her hair…her eyes so soft and full of life and intelligence. Here was this angel, in living form and he, the world famous doctor, who could perform miracles.

He, who had taken all that was believed about education and pushed it past its limits. He, who had sought to prove that reserve capacities of the human mind were endless, felt lost and forlorn. Powerless.

What if they weren't wrong? Even with all his genius, he had no cure for this. He would lose her, his Evelina, his love.

"They are wrong. It cannot be, Eve." Gentle, his voice did not waver or break. Not a single sliver or trace of doubt in it, even as it ran needles through his heart. No, it could not be true. She was too young. It could not be her time yet. She'd had some more worries lately. That was all.

No. He would not lose her. They must be wrong. "There is always a possibility of a mistake." The frown deepened.

"You must not trust them. What is called cancer could be something completely different. We will go together and will see again." His shoulders lifted with what she knew to be determination. "And in any case, it will pass." He seemed to be reassuring himself now, more than anything.

"Shall we continue with the work, Georgi?" She smiled and walked over to the desk, straightening the fallen papers.

When he had called her down to work, she hadn't pictured them spending the evening like this. Yes, she would tell him, and he would be sad for a moment, but then they would begin work, as always. Or, so she assumed.

Instead, it looked like he was going to sit in that chair all evening, staring at her. "What are you thinking about?" She asked him quietly. However, more rain fell against the window, *pat pat pat* like a little drum. It seemed fitting, overall, that the weather should be so grey. It matched the way she seemed to feel just then.

"Many things, I guess," Georgi answered after a moment. "You and I ... and our work." Strong hands gestured toward the study and the shelves that held almost the entirety of their lives. Books, papers, charts, reports, surveys...

Everything he had worked for, all of his life and yet, what was it now? While he would not, no, could not say it was empty, for his work was anything but empty. He did wonder at the certain lack of importance he felt for it, just then.

After all, all of it would still be here years later. What of them? What of her? Was she really to leave him to this world, alone? How would he continue, without her? Well, he wouldn't, of course. There wasn't going to be a 'without her' because she was going to be fine. Yes. That was all there really was too it.

CHAPTER 2

Heavy in the quiet city, rain drenched the ground as the nearly invisible sun touched the horizon, casting her fourth floor apartment into darkness. As night fell and the occasional trolley bus passed along Patraiarh Evtimii Street with the splashing sound of tires running through the puddles of summer rain, she looked out the window with a sigh. Now and again, a few cars here and there would drive by, jostling the silence as she contemplated her long, weary day. For the most part however, all was calm and thankfully, her home was no exception. After the usual, tiring day, her mother had finally drifted to sleep; somehow comforted in the unintelligible talk they had had together.

Something about stars in the trees, she had told her adamantly pointing out the nearby window. Of course, since it had just struck noon at the time, there were no stars. Or trees, for that matter, at least, none to be seen from the curtained glass that now reflected city lights and swollen raindrops. But to her mother, oh yes. There had been stars. Of course, there were, she had agreed quietly, out of the hearing of her small and far too impressionable boy.

He was also sleeping in his room now, quiet and tucked away from the world. That meant, to her joy, for just that little space of time, she was alone. It was the few, quiet times like this that she loved and longed for, to give her bedraggled spirit a break, even for a moment. In the midst of the ordinary hours of angry tantrums and fits, it was nice to just take time, even if it was so very few and far between. It was a rare miracle to steal such a moment but when she did, oh, it was lovely.

Now, only silence spoke to her softly as she sat, removed from the wailing of her mama and the yells of her angry little one that usually reverberated off walls of the apartment. It was comforting, to be alone but yet, as she watch the world go on outside her lonely little window, she found she wanted something more. Something … something sweet. Something beautiful. Something just for her, and no one else. To fill the ever-present ache that sat pitted in her thundering chest and gnawing. Without a thought to wonder what it could be, or the time taken to spare a cautious breath she reached for her salvation.

Smooth and delicate, yet strong, the old wood smelled like rosin and felt comfortable in her hand. Her violin. Dare she? Every day, it was everyone else. Never just her and her music anymore. A few notes from the instrument were unexpected and almost scandalous in the dim evening. Strong and warm in her chest, like a breath of summer air, she held the instrument close, drawing from it just the barest note or two. Tentative, she coaxed the instrument, whispering to it gently, almost soothingly. With each furtive note, lifting her to greater heights until all at once, it swept her away, like a great roaring ocean.

She played and played, put it down, corrected and played again. Each trembling note was perfection in and of itself. Each sound a single word from her soul, singing in sweet bliss with the violin as her voice. After a while, she paused and looked out the window. No noise could be heard in the small, timid street. Nothing but the rain. If she closed her eyes, she imagined she could hear it, singing back. Answering her as it fell on sparkling glass of the window. For the moment, everything was perfect and she sighed contentedly. If only everything could just stay like this, she thought to herself with a half-smile.

Then, all of a sudden, she heard it. The sound of heavy steps thumped and thundered loudly resounding through the apartment.

Her heart dropped to the basement and beyond with dread. Could it already be so late, she asked herself? He was home. Drunk again too, by the sound of it. She stopped playing and shivered with the sudden chill that swept across her shoulders and down her back.

Violently, if only to shatter her peace, the front door slammed open, shaking several haphazardly placed picture frames along the walls of the living room. From where she was sitting, she could hear everything perfectly. A wet sounding belch, then sound of s heavy bag dropping to the floor in the hall. Then the usual muffled mumbles of him talking to himself irritably as he took off his muddy boots. A few seconds more while she played out the scene in her mind, the curse sounded just on time and she could picture him stumbling over those boots as always. Even as predictable as it all was, each sound made her mouth dry and she wished nothing more than for all to be silent again. Clunk, clunk, clunk the steps echoed in her ears.

"Evo." She felt more than heard the rude snarl, with a wince. "Where are you?" Cringing at the rudeness, she sighed hard. The loud, course words sounded even worse as they reverberated off the walls of their tiny little kitchen. Dread paled her pink cheeks to the color of sour milk. "Is this my dinner? Where are you?"

Standing, she put the violin back in the case, slowly and without closing it. "Please," she prayed silently with a glance toward her mother. "Please," she beseeched as another crash came from the kitchen. For another second longer, she allowed herself to look out the window for one more moment before leaving living room. The door closed behind her softly. Though only a small two bedroom, the space from the living room to the kitchen seemed much longer than usual, now that he was home. Or, maybe it was only that she was walking so slowly, it took more time. She wasn't sure. The only thing she really thought of was the sound of dishes slamming around in her kitchen.

"Georgi, good evening, how was your day?" There was tiredness in her polite, patient voice. He ignored her and she was thankful, which only made it all that much worse. How horrible was this? She wanted to sound eager to see him and once upon a time, she would have been. After all, is that now how one should sound when seeing their husband for the first time in a day? So she thought, but couldn't stir herself for more than simple courtesy, no matter how hard she tried. Where had the time gone when she greeted him at the door, a smile on her face and warmth in her eyes? Or the time that the warmth was reflected back in his?

These days, usually, if she tried to catch his eye, she saw nothing but ice in those blue depths, when he would look at her, of course, most of the time he didn't. Where had the warmth gone? Didn't they love each other, once? That was how it used to be, in days passed. Meeting him at the door, her bubbling smile could have lit up the world at the sight of him, back then, and him laughing to see her. A beautiful, happy young couple who loved each other and loved themselves, that was a long, long time ago. Now? Now she had love for no one, save her mother and her son.

Now he didn't look at her, didn't even register her there, unless it was to shout at her. Otherwise, he didn't acknowledge her presence. To her mind, it was probably better that way. Taking out another bottle of Rakia, the tall engineer poured himself a glass full of the pungent liquid. The sight of it only made her mouth dry and she wanted to ask him not to, but it was gone in a gulp. Then he started talking away, talking of work, of the weather, of the time, of her and her mother.

Had he always been so harsh? Was it just recently his voice had become so unkind, his words unwelcome assaults on her peace? She took in the verbal assault with a bland expression, knowing anything more would only enrage him. If she was quiet throughout there was a good chance he would leave her alone after that and she wouldn't have to deal with him again that evening. Maybe, if she were lucky he would turn on the TV until time for bed. Then she could be left to her own devices.

Hopeful, she warmed up the meal, stirring from time to time and wondered how her boy was. Had he heard his father yell? Pray he had not. Oh, please that he had not. Let him sleep. Shameful though it sounded to her ears, she was much fonder of him when he was asleep, especially these days, now that his condition was worsening. It had only been a few years, perhaps three since her little one drank a big quantity of the spirit his father was so fond of. He hadn't been the same since. The doctors told her he had some sort of blood condition, which she had been desperately trying to cure with herbs and excursions but to no avail. Ill, irritable, and impossible to reason with, the boy was a living terror, much to her saddened dismay. Her husband seemed no better. Instead of correcting the boy, he usually encouraged him in acting out and tormenting her. What had happened to her life? Where was the warmth and happiness she fondly remembered from all those years ago, in the beginning?

She used to love her husband. Only nineteen when they married she remembered him as the attractive young engineer from Sofia he had been, always so kind and tender to her. When he wasn't drunk, of course. Then, after some time the little one came along and she settled to be a good mother and a wife. They were happy, for a while.

When they were younger, they went to Cuba. 1963. He was a talented, brilliant engineer who helped the local people. She remembered the time he and his colleagues had been building an irrigating system for the people. Everyone loved him and her both and they had loved each other more than anything. She went to the music academy to take private lessons from famous musicians, like Professor Iris Burget. He had been telling her as long as she could remember that she had been born with a voice that could change the world.

She never wanted to change anything, only make people happy. That was why everywhere they went, she sang for the workers or anyone else who wanted to listen. It made them smile, to hear her and they would laugh, sing, and complement the young couple wherever they went. She smiled thinking of the two of them as they had been.

Happy, happy faces brightened her memory, smiling at her performing the romantic songs of Schumann. In the middle of nowhere or a crowded street, a stage would be improvised and there she was, singing from the depth of her soul for all the beautiful people. She had been so alive! So happy! In Havana, they saw her off with a big concert predicting a bright future for the young Bulgarian opera singer Evelina Kotseva.

However, those days were gone and that bright future had dwindled into nothing, before she had time to watch it slip away. Now it was the lonely evenings, listening to her mother's lamenting whimpers and her angry boy rage at everything. What of her own lament? Where was that heart-shattering cry she yearned to let out? Stifled, she imagined by the day-to-day crushing weight of the world around her. It kept her awake at night and when she did finally sleep, it was what she dreamed of. The pain. The empty, aching loss of possibility and squandered time. She longed for the years to go back to a time when it was only her and her cherished music. She longed for herself; something she was being to realize was long, long gone. She longed to be something *more* but, there was simply nothing left for her to be. The years were gone, the time…irreplaceable.

In her memory, she couldn't even recall when it had all started. It seemed ever since she was a little child in Sevlievo, her world was nothing but songs and musical instruments. Lessons, sheet music, and bleeding fingers. She would practice and practice until she wanted to cry from the sore hands and blisters. Never the less, she continued until she was the best she possibly could be. It was all well worth it.

As long as she could remember, her love of music had been intrinsic part of her being. Years later she would write in the preface of her book: "And thus my interest in that "special" which was hidden in the art arose: in the sounds and the tones of the words, in the colors and the shapes, in the body movements and in the mimics; all that enchants us, surprises us, calm us and inspires us…" But as of yet, that was a million miles away, undreamed of and unrealized.

For now, it was the memories.

She had a good childhood, if different than most. Her mother had been brought up in another culture and time all together. Viennese by birth, she wanted her two girls to be accomplished young women. That wish was only spurred on as she watched the world raged around her. Wars, bombs, and people of all nations killed en masse. It was a horrible, painful time for the world and she was determined to give her little girls more than that. In 1939 Evelina was born and Hitler entered Poland and The Second World War was begun. The whole world felt the pain and loss of millions lives changed in one way or another by this huge event.

She barely remembered any of it, though on good days her mother could tell her some of what it had been like. Not that she asked often. The world she lived in today was hard enough. People died all the time and were just as scared now as they always had been. Yet life went on. People were married, babies were raised. She herself was a testament to that, she realized, thinking about her own family. As hard as life was today, how must it have been back then? Thinking about it, she wondered how it must have been to raise a child in those times. How terrifying was it? Could she have raised her boy, in a world like that?

A strident noise broke her thoughts, splintering them into a million tiny pieces. She stepped to the living room door, only to feel her face go numb with sudden shock. "No, no, no!" Her voice was just above the barest whisper as she watched with horror. "Not again, not again…" Her beautiful violin was on the floor, snapping like dry wood under her husband's big feet.

Red faced and sweating, his eyes bulged as a large blue vein pulsed slightly in his temple. It had been a long time since she had seen him so enraged. Large hands picked the stringed instrument up off the floor, shattering it against the wall with several rude words. Pale, trembling and mute with horror she watched her precious possession torn to bits by the man who had once claimed to love her. Had that been so long ago, a small part of her cried silently as she made to turn away. She couldn't look at him anymore.

Her mother woke. She heard the startled wail from the hallway and ran back, only to see the old woman sobbing with some unnamed grief. Evelina stepped over to comfort her, only to see the little one came scrambling from the next room, laughing to see the vandalizing of the instrument. Now it was her turn to sob as she watched the boy join in on breaking her beloved violin.

Finally, he stopped; face almost purple now where he wiped the sweat away. She could see he was plainly enraged, more so than he had been in a long time. The walls rattled as he stomped over to the TV set and switched it on. Black and white light flashed across his blotchy face as he turned back to glare at her. In this light, he looked like a great monster, huffing and puffing, growling under his breath.

"I don't want any scraping here!" He screamed fervently, little droplets of spittle flying out from his rage-whitened lips.

"And this crazy one," she cringed as cruel hands gestured wildly at her poor mother. "In the kitchen! Now" Huddled in her little corner, rocking and mumbling to herself the old woman sobbed.

"I don't want to see her idiotic face while I am watching the news!"

Seeing the confused, sad eyes of her mother Evelina turned her back to her husband and went over to comfort the elderly woman. Oh, the pain. She felt ill. Sickened. Her head was going to explode with the rushing sounds as she watched her son dandling the abused violin, swinging it around by its broken neck so that the strings caught the air with a shrill whistle.

Where had the warmth gone?

CHAPTER 3

In an obscure, dim little corridor of the hospital, a queue of souls sat outside the small office. Anticipation tingled in the air, almost tangible as the clock ticked by. Some paced and rubbed their hands together, brows knitted with worry. Others sat calmly, sighing now and again as though breathing was some grudging obligation they would just as soon have gone without. It was overall a dreary place. Looking at it, you would have thought they were waiting for the very gates of hell themselves to open and swallow the waiting crowd for their own personal damnation.

In truth, they were all waiting for that one individual miracle to save them. Dark clothes, dark, cramped little lobby and worried faces. Quickly counting the many people in front of them, Evelina sighed. It seemed they were to be here a very long time, if they were to see the doctor today. Other people in front of them looked like they had been there a very long time.

Tired, but patient no one cared how long they had to wait. It was worth it to them and worth it to her to wait an hour or three. The whole city was talking about him. You couldn't go anywhere without someone whispering about him. Everyone talked about his abilities, his kindness, his caring that knew no bounds. From one end of her beloved city to the other, people were talking about Dr. Lozanov's love for the people.

The young musician smiled skeptically to herself, wondering if such a person really could exist. Or was it all just talk? In these desperate times, it was easy to make much of little, especially when it was all you had. She knew this and tried not to get her hopes up too high. It was hard. Harder than she had thought, when someone had first suggested she take her mother to see the man. How could she not be excited? He was her last hope. Not for her.

Were it just her, she could walk away from it all easily and free up the carefully coveted space she had taken for the day. However, it was her mother. Her mama had been suffering so much lately and now to make it worse, her husband had insisted on putting her bed behind a curtain in the kitchen. She had been getting worse day by day, sometimes going hours without speaking or sleeping. Instead, she just sat and stared at the wall in her little corner.

Everything else she had tried to aid the old woman had failed. She couldn't stand to see her suffer like this. Today. Today had to be the day that turned it all around.

She hoped today she could leave with some of that awe-inspiring brilliance others had been raving about. At least then, things would be somewhat better at home. The constant anguish from the little one would be no better, but at least it would be something. He was getting worse too, despite her efforts and his father certainly wasn't helping. That was another thing she had meant to see to today, she remembered with a frown.

They were almost out of the necessary herbs they used to treat the little one. If she didn't purchase more, there was no telling what his condition could lead him to. It was awful, to think about but she knew by the time they were done here for the day, it would be too late to go shopping for more. Tomorrow then. It would give her a reason to go out again, something she enjoyed when she could.

A day away from the house that wasn't spent sitting would be lovely. Her husband would be angry with her. Then again, when wasn't he? It would be all right and if it wasn't, she didn't care. Not today. Today was all about mama, whom she looked to with a fond, hopeful look. Her husband would simply have to be angry.

"Mama, are you chilled?" She asked quietly, fixing the blanket around the little woman with a sigh. She didn't answer, of course. Evelina frowned. It had been over two weeks since she had last spoken. It worried her greatly to see her mother reduced to this.

Somewhere, in the quiet little space, the sound of a radio began to play. She watched in awe as her mother lifted her head from it's stoop, listening to the tune that flowed through the still air. The sunniest Italian song "Che bella cosa una giornatta di sole" serenaded the waiting crowd and the musician smiled to see the look of recognition in her mother's eyes.

Could it be a sign? Oh, she fervently hoped so, feeling her shoulders relax from their tight, military like stance of anxiety. This must be a lovely place indeed, she realized, taking in the music with a deep breath. For the first time in a week or more, she actually felt hopeful. She smiled, eyes closing as the singer took her away off into another world.

The next two hours passed by almost lazily, floating along the clock as her mother dozed in her chair. Another hour and they were still waiting for their turn. The doctor was known to take his time with every single person who visited him, which to her mind was a wonderful thing. It was yet another reason they all spoke of him so well, his patience. Some had even said he would take over an hour on one person, if need be. He was just that thorough. She did not mind at all.

Determination held her to her seat, upright and alert. She wanted so desperately to ask his opinion and to help her mother. No one else had been able to. Every doctor she could find simply shook their head, as if her beloved mama were just a lost cause. She refused to believe it.

When there was a will, there was a way. She believed it. She had to and if it needed another four hours to wait, she would do so if only to have her mother seen. By now, it was already seven in the evening.

The whole clinic was almost empty, save the four patients who were still waiting for their turn. She wondered what they might be here for. They all seemed relatively happy, to her eyes. Some even talked amongst themselves, whispering the most miraculous stories about the good doctor.

"They say he is young but very talented, he can even hypnotize." One woman remarked astounded, fanning herself with her hand. As thick and humid as the air was in the small space, Evelina couldn't say she blamed her. It was dreadfully hot and they had all been there a long time.

"What is hypnotize?" A small young girl with flaxen blonde hair asked the old worker who had accompanied his wife for her visit. The old man shushed her gently.

"Don't say it out loud," he chided, old eyes looking around the small little space they all shared. "There might be someone overhearing."

Evelina smiled and thought about the great composers. Mozart, Debussy, Rameau, Beethoven…they could hypnotize as well. A flick of the wrist. A note scratched onto the measure and the mind was lost under the spell of the masters and their music. The audience in the concert halls glued to their velvet upholstered seats, mesmerized by the stunning performance of the Sofia symphonic orchestra. Such was the power of music. In and of itself, it was a powerful medicine, healing all who touched it. Truly, when she sang she was also somewhere in another world, in another dimension, far from the darkness of her home healed and whole again.

What about this man? Could a man, one single being have the same effect on his patients? Could it be that he could provide the relief her mother so desperately needed as music provide Evelina relief from her own cares. Could a man heal such a grievous wound in the mind? She wondered, listening to the speculation of her fellow patients as they continued to wait.

Finally, it was their turn around 8:30 pm. She knew her husband was going to be so angry when she finally got home. She winced to consider it, already seeing the big vein, pulsing in his red angry temple as he screamed at her. It was too late to regret now. She was knocking on the worn door of the doctor's office. It looked tiny from the outside and, as she knocked again, she wondered how it must be to work in such a small space, day after day. A voice answered, jolting her out of her musing as she put her hand on the cold metal knob.

It turned under her palm before she herself could open it and she stepped back. "Please come in and welcome." A tall man answered gently, smiling down at the two of them. Surprise plainly lit her eyes to see no nurse or assistant there to help the young man who greeted them at the door.

He did not have the look of someone who had been working for almost 12 hours nonstop and with all manner of patients, some of them quite seriously ill. In fact, she could help but notice that for all that she had done nothing but sit in a chair all day, he looked far better than she did. As they took their seats, he smiled at them and spoke softly. The tone of his voice sent a strange, pleasant chill up her spine.

"How are you? You look well, comrade!" He asked the old woman.

Astounding, much to the young musician's surprise and delight, her mother smiled back. Not just smirked or crooned, but actually smiled. It was the first time in several weeks Evelina had seen the old woman so happy. A strange, warm feeling settled in her chest. Every hour they had waited seemed like a faraway dream as they began to converse with the doctor. By all appearances, it seemed it had been indeed worth it. She just hoped she wasn't wrong.

He was 39, tall, well built with black curly hair greying at the temples and… shocking green eyes. Catching those eyes for the first time, she felt her heart quicken in her chest. As close as they sat, she could count the little flecks of gold and blue that made the most startling starburst pattern in the almost emerald irises. They were welcoming and sincere…so kind and she felt her heart glow warmly with sudden new feeling. Hope. It was the first thing she noticed that marked the man as one apart from all the rest.

Even after a long day, he looked at them as if they were precisely the patients whom he had been waiting for all along. Throughout the conversation, his tone remained even and light, yet interested nonetheless. Yet through the interest and that refreshing kindness, she couldn't help but notice something else. A very certain sense of dignity, she realized, coupled with a very gentle but firm distance that he established with them almost immediately. In and of itself, that was comforting because she knew that she was dealing with a true professional. Someone who would not let his emotions color or lead his judgment. It was a wonderful thing indeed.

The year was 1965. Evelina could not know at the time that the doctor who was talking gently with her mother and carefully addressing her as her closest relative had already written the first manual of psychotherapy in Bulgaria. It would only be many years later that students and followers alike would turn the pages of his book with fingers that trembled in awe as they read the man's brilliance and his name would be known throughout the world, alongside her own. That was years away.

For now, she was happy to be calm and encouraged in that her mother was going to be all right. Reassured, they left with a date for another appointment and a totally new sense of renewed hope. In fact, by now she didn't think hopeful or renewed were the right words to describe how she felt just then. Happy even, though she was for the first time in a long while seemed weak and pale in the light of her teary eyes as her mother smiled at her. Nothing mattered. Not the angry shouts she knew she would face once home or the rude words. Not even the humiliation she was in just a short while could dampen her spirit.

She had found a human being who would listen and consider the needs of her mother and actually care. More than that, she had found hope. A new light, shining and beautifully bright that sat warm and comforting in her pounding heart. She had found something to believe in and believed in him she did, this kind, and brilliant man. Perhaps it was the eyes…those shocking green eyes that had kindled something in her. Perhaps it was the thing itself, but she realized then that she had found something. Something she thought long dead. It wasn't much more than a tiny spark for now, but it held her warm and brilliant like a great fire as she carried it with her everywhere she went. What was this, this feeling? She wasn't sure, but whatever it was, she was glad to have met the man who gave it to her.

CHAPTER 4

Waving goodbye to his last patient of the day, Georgi sighed. It had been a very long, very hard twelve hours for the young doctor and while he loved his work, he was glad it was time to go home. Time for them to go home, anyway. He couldn't leave just yet because while others making dinner or spending a few quiet moments with their families before bed, he still had another two hours of work. Medical files needed to be organized and catalogued. New names needed to be put into order while old patient information was updated and double checked. He was doctor, nurse, and secretary all for himself and there was still much work to be done.

With each piece of paper and every patient name, he saw the face of whatever tortured person who came to him, searching for a miracle from the hand of God himself. Usually, what they needed was someone to listen. Now and again, he would write a prescription or two, perhaps suggest something different be done in the person's life, but usually, all they needed was someone to hear them. To hear them was to love them and he loved every living being that walked into his office.

Old, young, dying or in the peak of health it mattered not to him for they had put themselves in his hands. They had trusted him and given him the responsibility of their well being. It wasn't something he took lightly and he found the weight of it constant, pushing him past any hurdle. Exhaustion, hunger, and thirst were secondary priorities while there was still someone counting on him. Even if it was only one. They were more than just patients to him. They were people. Living, breathing people who meant so much more than just a scribbled paycheck every two weeks and all the holiday benefits he had never taken.

He didn't have time for weekends or holidays. He didn't have time for much of anything. How could he? How could one fail at something when the only task was to love? It shouldn't have been a question at all and yet, with each new face, he felt just the smallest amount of fear grip at his heart. Cold in his chest, the question would arise as it always did and he would ask himself *what if this time, I cannot not help them?* What if this time, he would have to turn someone away without an answer? Without hope?

It was that fear that made him learn to cultivate and install a certain amount of distance with his patients. It was not a great thing, but enough to quiet the thought that terrified him more than he could probably articulate, were he to try to voice this fear. Not that he could of course. Not without opening himself to a point that he could share those deepest thoughts and as of yet, there was no one he trusted enough to do so.

To the rest of the world, he was the self-confident doctor who feared nothing and he could not afford for people to think otherwise. He would let nothing soil his reputation and therefore possibly risk the relationship he had with his patients. Not even the threats on his life, the scorn of his work or the whispers behind his back from his supposed colleagues. None of it.

Nothing would stand in the way of his work or his people. However, that also meant that he could trust almost no one. Perhaps one friend here or there, long ago but today? No one. So while he was never cold, or unkind; it was not in his nature to be so. It was enough to hold them away so that he did not become so attached as to have the pain crush him so horribly. It helped some, and while the fear never left, it at least made it easier to cope with.

Overall, it made for a rather lonely life and he longed to finish so he could go home. Pushing the file cabinet shut, he locked it tightly. The second to last key on the ring of many sparkled in the lamp light while the others jingled in its wake.

With all the lights cut off and one last door to lock, he shrugged off his crisp white coat and donned his jacket. The last thing to do was wave goodbye to the custodian and his soggy mop bucket before heading out the door. It wasn't much of a trip home, but the breeze was a nice change from the stagnant office air and he smiled, taking a deep full breath.

Narrow streets lit by quivering lamp light led to plush certain of greenery that cloistered his little apartments. He whistled a sunny tune and waved hello to a man walking his dog. From the door to the fence line of trees it was nothing more than a few paces over crunching clumps of silver leaves that clogged the walkway to his front steps. He was home. The brick and mortar building never looked so appealing, dappled in the silvery moonlight and waiting for him.

"I am here," he called, keys jingling in the doorknob. Silence choked his ears as he stepped over the threshold to the darkened stairwell. It bothered him not at all however as he had seen at least one light on in the upstairs window. Someone was up and he hastened up the stairwell to discover who it was.

It didn't take but a moment for him to find out and a smile broadened his tired face as he stepped into the bedroom. Settled on their little bed, nose in a book as always, his wife sat completely ignoring his presence until he placed a gentle hand on one dainty foot that sat, peeking out from underneath the blankets.

"Did you not hear me call when I came in?" He asked eyes lit with warmth as he smiled at her. Even after years of marriage, his heart still lifted to his throat at the sight of her, like a schoolboy with his first crush. Even after a long day, he found himself rejuvenated and happy just to be near her, his beautiful little wife.

"And if I did?" He wasn't sure if it was the words themselves that made his smile fade just a bit, or the tone.

"Well," he pushed it out of his mind and smiled anew. Today had been too long a time to let a little thing ruin his good mood. "I was wondering if you wanted to come downstairs and eat with me." He said quietly, pushing his glasses up where they had fallen down his long nose.

"I have already eaten." She replied, never moving her face from in front of her novel. That only made him more resolute and with a playful smile, he plucked the volume from her hand in with a grin that belied his exhaustion.

"Now," he dimpled at her, eyes twinkling with boyish delight. "Even so, will you not come down with me? I have been at work all day and have missed you very much. Please?"

"If you missed me so much," she began, snatching the paperback from his hands. "You would not have been out so late."

His heart fluttered weakly and seemed to stop for a moment as his smile faded altogether. Surely they were not to go through that again, he hoped, hurt but not wanting to show it. Sitting down on the bed beside her and removing his shoes, very slowly, he wondered what to say. It was obvious she was angry and he could understand why, but he could not be sorry for being out so late because that would mean being sorry for working. That he could not do.

"I wish you would not snap at me so," he said quietly, moving as if to hold her hand but stopping as she drew away. "You know I have very many people come to see me. Would you have me turn them away?"

"Is it so many?" She spat, finally flinging the tawdry fiction to the side. "Or only one? What sort of diagnosis do you give to people so late in the evening?"

Now it was his turn to be angry at the outrageous implication, though he would not admit it to her. "We have been through this before," he began calmly only to be interrupted as she continued her accusations.

"Oh yes we have been through it many times and I still cannot see how they keep you there so late, unless you are choosing to stay because of some woman." She crossed her arms now in that stubborn sort of way that told him she was not going to calm down anytime soon.

He knew her too well and knew that the way she held her little jaw and jutted out her shoulders meant that he would be sitting here for a very long time. There would be no discussion. To her mind, he was in the wrong and that was the end of it. There would be no argument.

With that painful realization and a heavy, heart sore sigh he stood. "Perhaps it is best if I eat by myself, tonight." The doctor said, keeping his voice as even and calm as possible.

Closing the door before she could say anything else, he sighed, strong shoulders lifting with the deep breath. It made his heart ache to think she thought so badly of him, trusted him so little as to believe that he would be unfaithful. Had they not been together years? Should she not know him better than that, by now? No, he undeniably realized.

While she might not know him any better than that, he knew her far too well to even ask such a thing. She had always been a resentful creature but over time, the pathological jealousy had gotten worse. Tonight however was the worst he had ever seen it and it saddened him to it see her so angry with him over nothing at all. If he were to be spending any amount of time with a woman who was not his patient, it would be here! How could she not know that?

In the beginning, it had not been like this at all. When he closed his eyes tight, he could still remember that light, airy feeling in his chest when his roommate at the time had introduced them. She was a high-school senior and he was in his last year at the university.

While studying one night as usual, he had abruptly been interrupted by Slavcho Denisov, his friend and roommate who had insisted the young student come meet his sister. He did not want to he had grumbled at the young man who know the medical student was terribly behind on his essays.

"They are due day after tomorrow," he had told him urgently even as he allowed himself to be coaxed up and out into the main house of their shared dorm room. Then he saw her.

She was tiny, black-eyed and tender faced much like his mother. So beautiful. He even remembered the way her curly hair framed that delicate little face as she smiled at him from across the tiny room.

"Georgi, this is my sister Stefanka." Denisov had said, smiling as pleasantries were made. From there, he would have usually gone back to his room and spent the rest of the night buried in his studies and writings but once he laid eyes on the girl, he found himself unable to leave.

Instead, they had spent several hours talking about his ideas. His plans, his work, and where he was currently in his studies. Not only did she listen, but seem legitimately interested. He had been flattered, charmed even and by the time the young woman was saying goodbye, she had spent more time with him than with her brother.

"Goodbye," he had sighed as she left, doe eyes glassy through his spectacles, something his roommate had teased him endlessly about.

Joking aside, for the young psychotherapy student, it had been instant love. Within a week, he had asked her to dinner with him and from there it was not long before they were married, despite protestations from both his family and hers. A beautiful wedding to his beautiful girl. Both of them just out of school and happy together. He had been so proud.

Was that so long ago? He wondered pushing cold leftovers around on his plate with a heavy heart. Where was that sweet girl he had talked to all those years ago? Now in her place was a cold, sharp woman who hurled blistering insults and wild accusations his way, no matter what he did.

His sweet girl was gone. This woman? He did not know her anymore and the more time he spent with her the more he wondered if he even wanted to. How could she think he was seeing a woman so late at night, when she knew how much his work meant to him? He had given his vow to her. Made her a promise and if anything she should know he could never just throw that away for some other woman. Besides, even if he had an inclination to do so, there was no woman around who he could possibly find interest in.

A sudden image of the young woman who had brought in her mother to see him came to his mind for a moment. Just as clearly, as though she had actually been there he saw her, smiling at him with those gentle eyes and then the image faded. *What a strange time to think of her, in the midst of all this,* he frowned. Completely unsettled by the whole thing he scraped the rest of his dinner into the garbage, shaking his head all the while. It had been a very, very long day and it did not seem to be getting any shorter any time soon, unfortunately.

Still frowning over it all, he made his way up the stairs once more. This time however, he did not go to his room, but to his son's to check on him. Thankfully, it seemed the boy was asleep. Blissfully unaware of the goings on between his parents, he slumbered peacefully, completely ignorant to the way his father tucked him in or leaned down to kiss him goodnight. This was good, Georgi thought smiling a little at the cute little look on his sons sleeping face. He was glad to see him sleep so soundly.

At the tender age of ten, it wasn't right for the lad to hear such things between the adults. He should have better things to think on, like schooling or his friends. Not the pointless bickering of adults. Leaning down to look his son over, he smiled to see the boy's sweet little face, so much like his own and yet, not. Here and there, he could see himself in the child but other times he could see his wife, that also made him smile at least, for a moment. He was a fine boy and would grow up to be an even finer man, given time. The doctor was sure of it.

The doctor and his wife had both done their best to make sure the lad had the best they could give him, even in these troubled times. They had done well together, he thought with a half-smile. Thinking about her made his heart sink just a little. They had done well, at least, when they weren't fighting like cats and dogs. Ruffling the tufts of dark hair that fanned out on the child's pillow, he leaned down to kiss his boy goodnight once more and stood before making his way back to his own bed.

The light was off now and she had her back to him, but he knew well she was not asleep. She was too stiff in her posture and to neatly placed on her own side of the bed to actually be unconscious. He sighed sadly. Pondering for a moment or two, he wondered if he should say something. Perhaps, try to comfort her? He crossed his fingers behind his back with one hand while the other placed itself on her shoulder. Without a word, she shrugged him off, vehemently pulling away and resituating herself out of his reach.

There wasn't much else he could do, he guessed. If she wanted to talk, she would. He knew well that not much would stop her if she had something to say and if she didn't it was just better to leave her be. She would speak in time, or not, as she choose, so he thought she never did. The night waned, giving way to morning and though she was already awake when he made his way downstairs, she said nothing to him. Even when he had went to say goodbye, landing a kiss on the dark hair that curtained her temple, she ignored him.

The walk to work was a slow one. His mind was clouded and muddled. He hadn't rested well at all and knew he looked tired. Now and again, he would crack a smile for the few individuals out so early in the day, but thankfully, they were rare. Maybe today would be a busy one and he would have plenty of work to take his mind off the ache in his heart. Even better, maybe they would not be busy and he would be able to rush home early, showing her that he did not stay late out of infidelity. Maybe, but he doubted it.

Keys jingled as he unlocked his office for the day and he stretched hard before plastering his usual confident smile to his tired face. So, he was tired and maybe he was hurting...but so were others and so long as they were hurting, he would smile if for no other reason than to show them that it would be all right. Even if he didn't always believe it himself.

CHAPTER 5

❧

In the three years that had slipped away without a moment's notice, much had changed for the young Bulgarian musician, Evelina. After leaving her job as a bank clerk, she was now working in the Sofia directory of music as a singer. It was an enjoyable occupation in and of itself, though it often left her feeling empty and dissatisfied. She yearned for something else, something...more.

Not only did she want to improve her technique and performance but it was hard to shake the feeling that something else was calling to her. Daydreams frequently carried her away too far off Leipzig and Vienna to study with the great masters as crowds of people cheered her on. It was disappointing to be brought back to real life and find her crowd of onlookers was only a handful of student singers. It wasn't always easy to remember the she was still in little Sofia and not off on some grand adventure.

Still, regardless of daydreams, she was contented enough, if a bit lonely. With the divorce recently finalized, the separation of her household and the recent passing of her mother still fresh, life was a new prospect altogether. She was no longer a wife, married to a man, but a divorced woman living with her child. Members of the communist society that once greeted the talented singer with esteem now passed her on the street without a second look, or avoided her outright. To be divorced was akin to being a leper in their eyes; a disease that damage the carefully constructed idea of what a family should be.

Yet another harsh reality was life in her country today, something she greatly lamented. Not only was it harsh, but it added to the awful sting of emptiness that was the loss of her beloved mother. At times, she forgot altogether that the old woman was gone. After all, it had been such a sudden thing. One minute, she was waving goodbye to Dr. Lozanov after an evening visit. The next, she was cold in her bed the next morning, peaceful and smiling like a little child. It was a great shock, for the young musician and the doctor both.

After three solid years of careful treatment, the old woman had improved remarkably. Completely removed from her old, downtrodden self and had even begun to contribute to the house chores with a smile. The doctor was a light in her dim life, in all aspects from her mother to her boy who seemed to flourish under the gentle influence of the older man. Now all of that had come to a dramatic halt in the blink of an eye and she was left with only herself and her boy.

Of course, Dr. Lozanov still dropped by now and again to check on them but it just wasn't the same. That made it very lonely both within the new home and without. It was a contrast, watching the green-eyed physician interact with her family so calmly as opposed to shouting at them like her husband had. Even more so to realize how different two men with the same name were. It had been somewhat shocking to her to discover the good doctor's first name was Georgi, the same as her husband. First names were the only thing they had in common however, she noted, thinking about just how stark the contrast was between the two men. One was gentle, caring, and intuitive while the other was coarse and overbearing.

Not that she spent much time with either, anymore. She had not seen her husband at all in the months leading up to their divorce, nor had she seen him since the event that was concluded in a matter of a quick quarter hour. A half an hour drive, 5 minutes to wait for their turn, 15 to speak to the judge and a quick scribble on paper. 14 years of her life were now null and void, gone to better days. Now, it was her and her boy.

All was well, seemingly and life went on as usual. The summer class she had enrolled in was going along smoothly; the concert hall was doing well. In fact, they were doing so well that a concert had been scheduled. The last minute solo she had half willingly been goaded into wasn't bad either. Unlike her fellow performers, who passed the days leading up to the event hyperventilating, she was perfectly calm about the whole thing. After all, what could be better than working in her beloved concert hall, as a soloist no less? It was her fondest dream come true. Years and years of careful study, playing her fingers to the bone and her voice to a mere whisper had groomed her for just this purpose.

Even with that strange...empty feeling, pursuing her almost constantly. Just when she thought the feeling had passed, it was always there, gnawing at her insides in the quiet moments she actually stopped to consider what it might be. Otherwise, it was just a dull sensation in her chest she noted now and again, when she had time. Thankfully, time was a rare commodity anymore.

Like ice in a glass of warm water, the mild spring melted away into a beautiful summer and the month of the concert was upon them. People were rushing in many directions to check, recheck, and triple-check that everything would be perfect for opening night. Three weeks before however, she was taking in a gasping breath to steady herself.

Tonight was the night. Class was over for today and rehearsals were tomorrow evening. Oh, how exciting was it! Her heart tittered in her chest nervously all day as she planned exactly what she would say. Work had rushed her through the week so far, but tonight was her night off, leaving only one class left before she could go. Her pencil bounced off the wooden desk to the tick of the wall clock, counting for her. Tick, tick, tick. 8 pm struck and she was the first up, calmly turning her work in before saying a hasty goodbye. She stepped out into the stifling hallway where the few others here for night classes milled about, chatting with one another. If she was lucky, she had hoped to escape without being stopped. Alas, luck was not with her this evening. By the time she could leave, at least six people had stopped her, either asking her about the date of the concert or congratulating her on having been granted the title role.

Manners dictated she thank them all, with a demure little smile as she confirmed dates and times for those who had not heard. It was times like this, when not a moment's respite was even heard of that she missed her old job. Or perhaps she simply thought she did. She honestly doubted she could be happier and yet…somehow, something in her life seemed to be…missing. It wasn't anything she could put her finger on. Only a feeling.

It was not all so bad however. Her family was well despite the recent stress and her classes were enjoyable enough. She'd even made a friend in all the commotion, to her great surprise. In fact, that friend, who she was just on her way to see, was the reason she had been handling everything so well. A smile lit her delicate face as she thought about him. Truly, where might she had been had she not been able to turn to ask him in those desperate moments?

In the darker days that had followed his first meeting with her mother, the man had turned out to be not only a reliable physician, but also the rarest of friends. No matter the day or the hour she called upon him, he was *always* willing to listen; she knew she could speak to him about anything. It was hard not to be at total ease with the man, though tonight she found she was not so relaxed.

Nervous even as her clicking heels carried her down the long hallways, she rehearsed her carefully prepared speech repeatedly. She wanted to sound confident, but not too eager. It worried her that she might come of sounding too humble and but she didn't want to sound overly egotistical either. She'd been wrestling all day with herself about it. Never mind that the natural conclusion was to act natural. In her mind, she knew that but in her heart, she wanted to deliver her invitation with grace and utterly floor the brilliant doctor.

That is, if he accepted. Would he say yes? Could he, such a great man, even have time to consider such a request? She was no fool about it and knew he was more than busy. Just from catching him in the hall earlier today, she knew he had had a hard day already and that was several hours ago. She couldn't imagine how busy he must be, but she knew it was enough not to ask him then, even though she had desperately wanted to.

Instead, she'd waited all day, rehearsing, praying and being completely absent minded about everything. It was worse than being in grade school once again, chasing after the boy next door. It felt almost the same, this rush in the face and when she spoke to him, and the color rose to her cheeks, it too, felt like it did when she was only a child. The admiration she held for the man was anything but childish, which is why she wanted to desperately for him to say "yes."

Rounding the corner, she felt her insides give a jolt before rearranging themselves into a new order. The air crackled with an invisible electric charge as she drew a breath. Heels came to a *clicking* stop and all of a sudden, she was standing in front of his door before she even realized she was there. Had his office always been so close to that second German glass? Or had that long walk just seemed quick in the midst of her anxiety. It seemed her feet knew the way better than she did and good thing or she might have walked all night.

"In circles no less," She muttered to herself, laughing with a giddy chuckle at the thought.

Straightening her casual suit dress and taking a strengthening breath, she smiled and sent a silent half prayer above. It was now, or never had she supposed, tapping on the frosted glass door before she lost her nerve.

"Yes?" a pleasant, smooth voice answered from within the office. She smiled to herself to hear the deep tone answer her and hoped she would hear much the same very soon.

Opening the door, the young musician dimpled prettily at the tall man sitting behind the cluttered wooden desk. "May I come in, Dr. Lozanov?" She asked with perfect demure confidence.

"Yes, yes, of course," waving her toward what he had come to consider as 'her' chair, he grinned.

She returned the expression easily, though flushed and hot faced. How could a grown man make her feel like such a fool? She wondered as he stacked his never-ending pile of papers onto the hardwood desk.

"I was beginning to wonder if you'd forgotten how to get here." Green eyes twinkled at her merrily in mock rebuke as she took her seat.

The stuffed leather was cool and smooth against her hand where her fingers rested on the sloping wooden arm. Brass metal tacks that held the fabric caught her eye in the lamp light where they gleamed from under her fingertips.

"Oh, I'm sorry I've been terribly busy…" Flushed at the idea that he had noticed her absence she found herself speechless.

Had he missed her all that much? How did he have time to think of her, in the middle of all that important work? After all, the director of his own institution surely had more to do than keep up with wayward musicians.

"Ah," She fumbled over her words, still flushed. The thought of music reminded her of her original purpose for visiting in the first place.

"How are you? " Starting a bit at the sound of his voice, she watched the doctor dandle his ink pen with absentminded fascination. What noble, gentle hands he had, for such a strong looking man.

"Quite well," she replied folding her hands in her lap as her heart leaped to her throat. Calm, she told herself. Calm. It was only small talk. No reason to get all upset.

"And Julian? How is he?" Fine of course, she wanted to say but stumbled over the words almost bashfully. This was ridiculous, she realized, straightening her back with a momentarily determined frown.

"He is also quite well," the frown softened instantly as she caught his eye turning into a sudden and brilliant smile. Gratitude shining plain in her eyes, she sighed. In truth, her mother and son had never been better, thanks to the doctor's diligent care over the past three years of constant house calls, phone conferences and of course the nightly visits to his office after class.

"I am glad to hear this." He smiled himself now, green eyes warm like spring grass where the sun had taken off the chill of winter. "And what about yourself?" He chuckled, making her breath catch. "What has kept you so busy you stay gone for three weeks?"

"Well," Fiddling with the fold of her skirt, she sat helplessly as her cheeks took on a delicate pink. "That is what I have actually come to speak with you about, this evening..." She trailed off, taking a deep breath before swallowing hard.

"Well, go on," He said encouragingly, smiling all the while.

That made her feel a little better, at least and she relaxed ever so slightly. "Well, I..." She crossed her fingers behind her back for luck and sent a silent prayer heavenward. At this point, she felt as though she'd truly reverted to being a teenage girl again as opposed to the 30-year-old woman she was. "You know I am working at the concert hall now, yes?" She asked, knowing it was an unnecessary question even as he nodded.

"We are currently organizing a concert and... I shall be performing a solo." Pausing now, she waited but for what she wasn't sure. It just seemed the appropriate thing to do. Perhaps for her heart to slow or her palms to dry where they sat moist and clammy on her knees.

"That is wonderful, Evelina," The doctor's smile was warm and encouraging as he beamed at her. "When is this to take place?"

Three weeks' time, which was wasn't long at all, though suddenly it seemed years away. Decades even. "The first of the month." She told him, feeling her own lips turn up at the corners at the sight of his smile, contagious as it was. She wanted nothing more than to see that smile, shining from the audience as she sang for the whole world. Oh, please, please say yes.

"I was thinking perhaps," Here it went, all or nothing. "If you were not busy you would like to come view the performance?"

There. She had done it. Weeks of building up for just this moment and it was over. Now it was up to him to turn her down or accept, which she anxiously waited for him to do.

"Perhaps," she watched his brow pucker with concentration as he pondered the question. "I am uncertain of my schedule, as of yet." No surprise, after all, the director of an institute probably had little if any time to spare, she imagined.

"Will you let me answer you later, when I better know where things stand?"

Nodding, she smiled masking the disappointment that seemed fit to crush her, though she knew it was not the end of the world. While it wasn't the 'yes' she had hoped for, it wasn't a negative answer either. So it could have been much worse. She would just have to wait a bit longer to find out than she had hoped. That was all and happy nonetheless she sighed contentedly, feeling a soft, *warm* sensation settle in her chest.

Even in the quiet, neither one saying a word to another, the silence was somehow more fulfilling than a hundred words with a handful of people. Perchance this companionship had her heart all a flutter and her eyes bright as she looked up at him finally.

"It's getting late, you know…" It was. Somehow, time had passed unnoticed and she had been here nearly an hour already. The babysitter watching her young boy would want to go home soon, meaning she needed to hurry as not to keep her too late.

"Is it?" As always, he never seemed to notice the time and was surprised as always.

Did she perhaps see just a fleeting glimmer of disappointment as he glanced at the clock on his wall? Maybe a flicker in that bright smile of his? She wasn't sure. It could have just been her imagination. Wishful thinking or a reflection of the sudden loneliness that threatened to consume her they both stood. Had she asked, she was certain he would have said he felt it too, though she didn't. It just rolled off her back as it did every night she had to leave, somewhat comforted in the fact that she was not alone in her loneliness.

"You will be by to visit day after next, yes?" She asked quietly. What long time away that was, she realized at his slow nod.

"Here," he stepped in front of her, opening the door with all the grace of a courtly gentleman. "Let me walk you to your car."

"Thank you, Dr. Lozanov," she said quietly.

"You are very welcome, Evelina."

CHAPTER 6

§

It was a warm June afternoon when the final rehearsal for the concert was finally completed. Life as anyone knew it was now a constant rush of hurrying and excitement, as the final preparations were made. Stages were set, instruments check and rechecked by their harried owners while vocalists could be heard humming their numbers nervously under their breath. It was both wonderful and terrifying.

As the title character and main soloist for the evening's production, Evelina was feeling the pressure more than usual, but unlike her fellow performers, was handling it well. She had been groomed for this moment and many others like it since she could walk, was quite used to last minute nerves. It was just one more day in the life of a young musician.

"Aren't you anxious?" One of the young tenors asked her, just as they were stopping for lunch.

Yes, she was she admitted quietly. What she didn't say was over what. Certainly, the concert was an important thing and of course, she took it very, very seriously. On the other hand, she'd never been quite this nervous over performing. Was it, she wondered, the usual stage nerves for opening night, of was there perhaps something else going on here? Of course, it had nothing to do with the possibility of a certain doctor making an appearance that evening, no, not at all. That's what she told herself anyway as she went about her day in a haze of last second running around.

Time passed quickly enough for the little group as they went about their individual tasks, but it was obvious that everyone was nervous. Thankfully, for them, there was only a few hours left to wait before the big moment. As the hour drew ever nearer and the anxiety rose, Evelina couldn't help but pray silently for all involved. It wasn't as though she thought she would do poorly. She knew her team better than that. It was everyone else who wasn't so sure, despite a brilliant rehearsal and she knew it was mostly because of the waiting.

Finally, when it was time for everyone to go home and get ready, she watched everyone relax for a moment before charging out in mass, some hurrying toward their separate vehicles while others traveled on foot. That left only her to make her way home, with the light, airy step of someone who was very, very excited.

Once back in her apartment, she was able to relax fully as she prepared herself for the evening.

With little to do in the way of getting ready and even less to clean the already immaculate house she decided a few runs through her solo would entertain both herself and her boy as they waited for the sitter to arrive. The little fluttering in her heart made her jump in place, but her voice was strong and sound nonetheless. Somewhere nearby, she was certain she could feel the spirit of her mother, watching over and encouraging her, just as she had all those years before at her first recital.

Wiping a tear away where it crept down her cheek, she sighed. The sitter was knocking on the door and it was time to leave. Closing her eyes, she allowed herself one last deep breath to gather herself, before opening the door to the young blond girl who lived next door.

"Come in dear," She smiled. It didn't take but a moment before all was settled and she was leaving, waving goodbye to her son with a smile.

Stepping out and closing the door behind her, the musician couldn't help but smile at the vision that was her beautiful city. Gracious in their embrace as she stepped out into the light, the well-groomed streets that lead to the concert hall were near gleaming from the caress of the warm sun. Thankfully, her flat was not too far a walk to the cathedral.

"Ah," She sighed. How beautiful her Bulgaria was that afternoon. Contented to look upon the everyday scenery that passed her by, the young woman couldn't help but smile.

While the concert was still about an hour away and she had a time to do as she pleased, she couldn't helped but be drawn to the cathedral that would house the evening in less than two hours. Perhaps it was the overwhelming sense of inspiration and the need to reflect on it in the quiet. I could have also been the feeling of safety she felt inside the large building; despite the fact, it actually wasn't safe at all.

Never mind that it was the opera house, as well as a religious building. To any party stalkers that could be lurking about, if she was seen entering the building for something other than singing, it could be dangerous. Yet still, it called to her. She looked around, frightened for a moment as a wild streak of disobedience struck her spirit.

She was going to go in anyway, regardless. It was part of the inherent stubborn streak her mother had warned her about for years. Usually, she managed to curb the desire and give in to the safer route. Not today. Today, she was going to go pray in her cathedral.

However, she was not going to be stupid about it. Quickly putting on the cardigan, which she carried in a little bag slung over her shoulder, she entered the big building and looked around carefully. Checking to see if anyone had noticed her she sighed and relaxed. Seemingly, the large cathedral was empty, save herself. Alone, she stepped through the threshold fully and felt the entire world slip to fall and fade away behind her.

Gone was the drowsy afternoon, forgotten for better things as she took in the greatness that was the holy building. While she had spent almost every day in that self same piece of stone architecture for a good three solid months, it seemed different now that she was alone. Sterile yet warm and utterly inviting, the air seemed to embrace her as she took one, slow breath after the other. Into the stone hall, she walked. Quiet and soft, not wishing to disturb the peace of the building in her haste. Even with no one else around, anything less than that would have been disrespectful.

After purchasing a few candles and making her way to the altar, she felt a sudden chill rush over her. The enormous cathedral was silent. Mass was to begin at five o'clock and yet, not a single living soul could be seen or heard. A few candles flickered in a nearly unfelt breeze, casting vague shadows upon the ornate walls. Otherwise, all was silent stepped close to the flush of warmth and flickering candles that bathed the graceful altar. Carefully placing herself in front of the big icon of Christ she closed her eyes began to pray silently. In that late afternoon stillness without anyone around, Evelina felt almost as if someone was trying to tell her something.

First a quick, but heartfelt prayer for her mother, then one for her son. In another day, when she was not in a hurry for time, she would have liked to take more time for them but today would just simply not allow it. So, off she went, quickly but silently, going through the ornate motions of the ceremony and prayer with slowness in her heart, if not in her actions.

First, the white icon of Christ, to stand humbly in front of his feet, then to the Virgin Mary she went, praying silently all the while.

Suddenly, a miraculous thing happened. Within the quiet peace that had settled over her, she imagined she could hear herself singing

Schubert's Ave Maria. Tears of yearning pricked her closed eyes as she felt her soul reach out and beyond her body, rising to give her gratitude to the blessed mother and fill gaping silent space with the sounds of her tender soprano voice.

To let the great dome of Alexander Nevski Cathedral resound with the ringing of her joyous tone and prosper in her spirit's delight. Oh yes, she wanted it. She yearned to hear her voice pronounce the lyrical prayer without the fear of a party stalker having seen her in church. What could be more wonderful than that, she asked almost aloud as she prayed to the benevolent face that looked down upon her.

Then a powerful sound struck her ear, jerking her eyes open with slight shock. It was some piece of music, sung by the Choir of the Cathedral. Brought her back from her dreaming, yet vivified even after the spell was broken she stood completely still. Listening to the sounds around her, she smiled, softly. In truth, while she would have loved to hear her own voice resound through the grand architecture, there could be nothing more majestic than those male voices with all their devotion. Settling to pray once again, she stayed a bit longer, and then silently excused herself, leaving as carefully as she had entered.

Now, in less than 45 minutes time, she would be singing and she hurried from the building to make way for those who were already filing in to ready the stage. With a much quieter heart and a lift to her chin that had not been there before she took off her cardigan and arranged herself once more. Only then, with her head held high, did she make her entry into the stone building once more. The nervous energy of the afternoon now vanished, replaced with a new sense of peace that settled over her spirit as she took her place, ready and waiting...

Nearly a half hour later, she sat behind the velvet curtain breathing easily as she surveyed the crowd. The concert hall was near bursting with anticipation both behind and beyond the velvet curtain.

Shimmering silk dresses and fine suits practically gleamed in the dim of the lamp light, like a display of fine jewels set out to be gawked at. Prancing peacocks and preening pretties socialized with one another as they waited for the evening's entertainment. Party members accompanied the comrades from the Soviet delegation. Old ladies puffed out their bejeweled shoulders like angry birds while repressed intellectuals conversed quietly in nearby corners. Students and officials alike stood shoulder to shoulder as everyone made nice for the sake of the evening's entertainment.

Ordinary people who did not wish to rub shoulders with the party members sat quietly with their families had come to return once again to the times when they could all freely listen to the classical music, discuss controversial ideas, and pray in the church. It was a rare, somewhat frightening sight to see them all together. Fear mingled with mildly veiled contempt charged the air with an almost tangible shock. Had it not been for the great music they had gathered for that evening, you never would have seen such people together. Even with the obvious distrust from all sides of the political scale, not a single person there would not miss the performance of the young soprano for the world.

Then, there was him.

As he entered the concert hall, she felt her heart drop to the floor. The sudden quiet chattering of all the little groups ceased instantly and silence reigned supreme throughout the antechamber. No one moved as the tall man stepped across the floor to his seat, taking it with a gentle, almost apologetic manner, as though somewhat upset for causing the disturbance and yet he almost seemed not to notice.

How anyone could be unaware of the sudden silence, was beyond her as all eyes landed on the doctor who now sat quite placidly, thumbing through the program for the evening. Then a wave of commotion splintered the quiet, making her draw the breath she hadn't realized she was holding. Audacious whispers flowed from flapping mouths with speculative fervor while, fingers pointed at the doctor without shame.

Some laughed openly while others stared in what couldn't have been anything else but awe. Even the old women were craning their necks to have a gander at him, through their glittering opera glasses. It must have been dreadfully uncomfortable for the young man, having all those people make such a fuss over him simply being there, but to any who looked at him, he didn't seem to notice.

She on the other hand was a bundle of nerves watching the goings on from her vantage point, tucked away, and waiting in the wings. To be quite honest about it, she thought she would have been less nervous had the near rude attention been directed toward her! Certainly less offended by the outright rudeness that certain people were displaying, she noted with a frown. How inconsiderate could they all be?

Fortunately, enough for all involved, the lights dimmed to nearly nothing as the first performer was called to the stage. Only half watching the young tenor at his work she wondered at the feeling of joy that flooded her being, tinting her cheeks the most delicate of pink. He came! Now that all was quiet, it was easy to forget her upset from a moment ago as it was shadowed by pure delight. All the worrying and fret over whether or not he would attended, for weeks upon weeks it seemed and yet there he was.

After her tentative invitation, she had wondered if he would, could even consider it. While she had hoped and dreamed with all her might, she didn't really expect it…But there he was carefully listening to the arias from La Traviata. Inhaling deeply, she put her hand on her heart, as if still the drum that beat within her chest, thundering like a grand storm at the sight of him. And what a sight it was. Gone was the usual doctor's coat and professional appearance. In its stead was a jet-black tuxedo that fit him like a glove as he sat, subtly beautiful in contrast to all the prancing popinjays that flocked around him.

Not only was he beautiful to look at, but beautiful to *see*. Calming, even she would say, watching him from afar.

What was it that made the man seem to exude such light and calm? Such…warmth? Was it his dignity? Or perhaps his position. After all, he was so young and already a director of an institute as well as an influential voice in almost any circle he stepped into. Then there was of course his self-confidence, as bright and beautiful as the smiled that gleamed on her face where she watched him.

Maybe it *was* because he was moving in all circles, accepted, envied, and talked about? No, there was something else, she realized quite suddenly. Something inexplicable that she could not explain. Intangible yet plain, the difference set him apart from all others, all competition blown away without a chance. There were no other men like Doctor Georgi Lozanov.

Looking at him more thoroughly than she had before she studied him carefully as she would have a new piece of sheet music, trying her best to define exactly what she was seeing. Perhaps, thinking about it was the strong air of conviction the man had that plainly said he thought what he was doing was right. Yes, that must have been it.

He had some hard times, she had heard people say. Sometimes in passing, he would mention a thing here or there to her to make her think that they were right. She didn't know for sure and certainly wasn't going to pry, thought, when it all came down to it, she didn't think she had too.

After all, in this day, who out there in the working world had not? Nonetheless, in such a small place, that was her beloved city it was hard not to overhear. People talked. Gossips could be heard in the grocery, at the library, at the pharmacy where she picked up the herbs for her boy and even in the waiting room, when she was still taking her mother to see him.

Stories flew wildly back and forth saying all sorts of things about the doctor that ranged anywhere from fantastic to completely outrageous. Yet he never seemed to care. To her, he always seemed to be in perfect straights. Was there ever a force that could be daunting to such a man? Not even the politics that swept across their part of the world seemed to sway him. He was still resolute, something that only endeared him to his people even more.

There was the something aristocratic about him as well, she noted, watching his careful movements as he shifted ever so slightly in his chair. Such poise and gravitas that was almost impossible not to see, if you were to spend any time with the man. Beyond that, she had noted what could only be described as an invisible veil of protection that graced his being, speaking of narrowly escaping nameless atrocities that had been in store for him. She would not be at all surprised to know he had escaped death once, if not more than that.

There, in all the elegance that could become a man stood a scientist who knew the importance of each signal and stimulus, each name that came to him in desperation. Green eyes, brilliant even in the semi dark carefully watched the performance, taking in each action or note with the air of a connoisseur sipping a fine wine. Those eyes that spoke of a genius that none could match. Such a great man, yet, he was here. For her. Not a patient, or a lecture. Not a meeting, or an intellectual discussion. For her.

The sudden realization struck her like a bolt of lightning. She knew it in her heart of hearts; he had come to see her. Feeling her hands tremble and her heart flutter into her throat she felt the privilege to fall in love at 30.

CHAPTER 7

Morning broke across his Bulgaria like the splash of warmth across the word. The sun was shining, the sky was blue, and children laughed as birds serenaded the cheerful city. It was a beautiful day to the rest of the world just waking while Dr. Gerorgi Lozanov had been at work for several hours already. This was nothing unusual to the young doctor. By now, he was used to rising before dawn to make the long trek to work, whether by foot or by car.

But even as beautiful as it all was and even though he was more than used to it by now, mornings were still very hard for Georgi, these days. Long nights and early rising before the sun had kissed the sky made for very little rest at night. And what sleep he did get was broken and fitful as he tossed and turned. In fact, he could really remember the last time he had a full nights rest.

But how could he? Especially now? He was so close to a breakthrough in his work that would essentially change everything. If he could just make this one last push, he knew it would change everything about his methodology and how he worked. If only! So, so close, he could taste it, yet he was constantly at a stalemate. No matter what he tried, the studies seemed to have reached the peak of their progression. Any attempt he made to farther them got him nowhere and even sometimes reversed the process.

It was all very disheartening, even discouraging at times. For the life of him, he could not seem to find the solution. Perhaps he needed a break, he had considered. Maybe a day off or at least an hour or two away from the work to give his mind a rest. It seemed like a well enough idea at the time, but he found it almost impossible. Wherever he was, there was his work and anything else he tried to do was spoiled by the constant need to scribble down some new idea or musing.

He needed something he could actually *do*. Something that would consume him so completely, he forgot his work entirely, if only for an hour or two. But what to do? Where could he go he was not constantly confronted by his work? It was his life, after all. Be it faces he knew well, stopping to speak to him in the street or some snippet of conversation making the wheels turn, he could escape.

Scanning his office full of its textbooks and charts, he sighed, praying for some kind of inspiration.

It seemed he could not escape the sea of papers. The study material had haunted him in his dreams for the past year and a half. Even when he slept, his mind projected the information into his slumbering head, like an incessant tape reel, reminding him how close he was and how far he had come. Unfortunately, when faced with ostensible stagnation, neither one of those things seemed like any progress at all.

Alas, to his wandering eyes the silent study revealed nothing. Not even a glimmer of hope was to be seen amongst the sea of papers. He sighed and folded his hands into his lap, resisting the urge to fidget. Such nervous jesters caused negative feedback, he reminded himself sternly. He certainly didn't need any of that.

Suddenly, a sparkle of gold flashed in the corner of his eye, catching his roving attention. Curious as always, he stood already reaching for the unknown object, plucking it from the immaculate ledge easily. The gilded, wax sealed envelope was surprisingly heavy in his hand despite not weighing much at all. As soon as he touched it, he knew instantly what it was but opened it anyway, wanting to hold it for himself.

SUGGESTOLOGY

"You are hereby invited to attend an evening of entertainment held at the Alexander Nevski Cathedral, on June 1st." He read the missive aloud, fingers stroking over the delicate gold calligraphy and smooth paper as he thought of the person who had given it to him. The first was it? That was day after tomorrow. Was this the chance he was looking for? Frowning, he sighed again, his breath a long huff of frustration. This would never do! He was supposed to be finding something to free his mind, not strain it farther. Not that the music would do that, per-say. The performer on the other hand.

The thought of the young woman made his chest tighten, ever so slightly. In the three years, he had known her the relationship between them had changed dramatically. First of course had been the careful understanding between a professional and a family member of one of his patients. Over time, what with constant visits between the two and late night calls for advice on any manner of things, they had become friends. Now this, something else altogether, though just what it was he couldn't say.

No matter what the difficulty, he had tried his best to be there for her throughout, including the recent divorce, which in turn helped him with his own sordid marital life. His own divorce was to be finalized within the week, something else that had been straining his tired mind. He was a mess, where as she seemed to be doing better than ever. It seemed, until the sudden passing of her poor mother. Even with his carefully cultivated detachment, it was hard not to be saddened by the passing of the old woman, whom he had come to care for very greatly over the years.

There was two traumatic events for poor Evelina to deal with, yet she stood stronger than ever, having risen up from the ashes of bitter separation like a golden phoenix in the flame. He on the other hand could only choke on the putrid smoke as he watched his own hearth fire wither and die after years of a committed relationship. All thanks to petty jealousy. What was his life coming to? Sixteen years of marriage... gone. He had tried so hard.

He would still have held on to them, despite the bitter atmosphere of his house, had his soon to be ex-wife let him. Even the dark backdrop that set the scene for every moment of his waking life could not deter him, no matter how daunting it sometimes seemed. The way he saw it, anything could be overcome, with enough time and effort. Then the final straw came. He'd just finished a fifteen-hour work day. Never before in his life had he been so tired and by the time he had returned home he wanted nothing better than to sleep. She had been waiting for him. Not even a foot in the door and she was there, her little face white with fury. He could tell she had been crying. "You are late again."

His long-suffering sigh was, mercifully, only internal as he reached out a hand to pull her close. "I am sorry, Stefanka." He said simply. He would make no excuses to her. She knew by now the price of his work, even if she chose not to believe it. "No!" Pulling away, she railed at him, her voice shrill and sharp. "You are not sorry. If you were sorry, you would not do this to me." She cried with her hands in her hair, delicate little voice cracking with strain.

He watched motionlessly as she stomped around their apartment, cursing him and all the supposed women he was ostensibly out with so late at night. Finally, after all the steam was blown off, he took her hand in his.

"Can we go to bed, please?" It was too late in the evening to argue and he was far too tired. "Please," he nearly pleaded, coaxing her up the stairs one-step at a time. "I have the day off tomorrow," he said quietly, his voice gentle as he silently prayed she would give in. "Maybe we could go out for a while and..." he trailed off, feeling her jerk away just as they reached their bedroom.

"Oh, now you decide to take a day off?" She hissed in the semi dark, her voice low so as not to wake their son, Boyan. "Maybe it is I do not wish to go out." With tired eyes that longed to close and a leaden stomach he sighed, this time letting his breath articulate the pain he felt inside.

"What is it that you want then, Stefanka?" He asked, knowing the answer before he had finished the near patronizing question. He had assumed she would then take on the dramatic posture of the actress she had never been, well up with more tears for a bit, and then change the subject back to his wrongdoing. Then, after a few more rounds of apologies, she would be settled for another week or two.

Not this time. This time she did none the above. In fact, she did nothing at all for a very long time, except look at him. When she finally did speak, he could not prepare himself for the words that came out of her mouth.

"I want you to leave your patients." She said simply. Just like that. As though it were such an easy thing to do. She just outright demanded it. Never mind what they needed. After all, since she didn't work, in fact, refused to work, it was all well fine and good for her to sit. She did not have to pay the bills or put food on the table for the two of them and their son. He did.

That was to say nothing of the obligation to his work, his institute, and his patients. Shaking his head, he slipped past her into the darkened bedroom, already undressing for bed. "You know I cannot do this." As if it was even a thing to do. Not only was it impractical, seeing as how money did not grow on trees, but it was also immoral. Those people needed him and he had a duty to them, if not to himself. But she would not hear it. Repeatedly, he had tried to tell her, but it was just beyond her understanding.

"Why can you not?" He flinched at the childish, whining tone her voice took on as he turned to look at her, still standing in the doorway.

It was then that he took a moment to look at her, really honestly look at her and his heart fell. This was not his wife. Not even a good imitation of her. The soft, gentle girl he had married was gone. Dead! Killed by this icy specter that stood before him robbing the man of life and love as each moment passed and yet…he could not turn away.

He doubted he ever would turn away, until he heard her speak. "If you do not give up your practice, I will tell the party you plan to defect."

It seemed the world had fallen away from his very feet just at that moment, following the color in his face as he was plunged into a gut numbing pit of disbelief. Surely he had missed heard her.

"What did you say?" The doctor whispered, lips numb as he met her eyes. What he saw there made him cold all over his body.

"I will tell the party you plan to defect." She said it again and he watched his vision darken for a moment before taking a hasty seat on the bed.

With that, she left, shutting the door with a heartbreaking click as he stared numbly at the floor. By this point, he had been up almost twenty-four hours. He was tired. Far beyond tired but could not make himself lay down. Not in their bed. Not here, where so much had happened. He doubted he would ever be able to sleep in the house again. Not after this.

He knew as well as she did that to tell the party such a thing, even untrue as it was would mean his death. Or hers. It wasn't as she would get off without being under suspicion. Not to mention the danger to their son. Oh, how foolish could she possibly be? Could she care so little for her family. Was she really so desperate to have him under her control that she would rather lose him altogether than have him as he was?

Apparently so. It saddened him to realize that after so many years, it was over. And what of him? Why was he incapable of holding on to someone, just once in his life? First, his mother. She had died when he was two. Sometimes late at night, when he was just falling asleep he thought he could remember the touch of someone soothing him to sleep. Tender eyes, smiling down at him as someone sang him to sleep…These were the things he remembered, in that period just between waking and sleep.

Then of course, there were his grandparents, who had raised him for the first part of his life after his mother had died. Those were his happiest memories. The little house on 66 "Oborishte" street had been his childhood home, for many years until his father had taken him away. Then he went to live with him, his new wife, and new daughter. Of all of that, his baby sister had been the only solace in it all. She had been the light of his life. Over time, he had come to love his father and new mother. They were not bad people, but he had missed his grandparents terribly. And now, what? They were all gone. All of them. And so was she. These thoughts sickened his mind as he stood up from the bed.

The plush, familiar carpet crumpled under his feet while an unnoticed breeze fluttered the nearby curtains. Through the open window, he could see his sleeping city, quietly saying nothing to him, in the darkness. What could be said, now? In an absentminded, half-sick daze he dressed himself once more just as he would have for work.

Without a word to her or even an acknowledgement as he passed her on his way out, he left, walking all the way back to his office. From there, he sunk into his stiff desk chair, whole body crumbling under it all. It was then that he knew. There was no holding on. No making this work. Despite it all, he knew what he had to do. He would have to divorce her. It was a very long, very hard, very expensive process and a bitter thing for all involved.

Even his son, whom he had tried to shield from the fighting and the woe over the last few years, could not escape. He was brought into the proceedings too, much to Georgi's bitter approval. Thankfully at least, it was all done rather quickly. Boyan had chosen to go and live with his mother and in just a few days; it would all be done and over. That was it. Sixteen years and what did it amount to? A few months, a pair of expensive lawyers and empty apartment.

That was it. Now it came down to this, an aching head and invitation to Evelina's concert. No. There really was no way around it. He just simply couldn't go; maybe another time, when he could think clearly; maybe when he was not reprimanding himself every time the thought of a certain young singer who made his eyes light up, especially in times such as this. No. Shaking his head, he placed the invitation back on the shelf and pushed it and Evelina out of his thoughts.

He would find something *else* to free his mind.

CHAPTER 8

W ithout many options, Georgi supposed the best thing to do for now was get back to work. Combing over notes, studies and psychotherapy textbooks, he set himself down to another few more painful hours of checking and rechecking something he could have easily recited in his sleep. It was all standard procedure for the young doctor and at this point he thought he'd be happier if he never saw it again. Obviously, however, giving up was not the way to solve the problem. Then again, neither was staring at it in a way that should have made the ink melt right paper, as he had been over the last month or so. First, he would reread what he knew, break it down to its base method, and build it back up again, weeding out all imperfections or unnecessary dealings. Then, he would do it all over again, until he wanted to scream.

And this would go one for a pair of days, until eventually, he would give in. Of course, the occasional sighting of Evelina in the hallways of the university didn't help. Nor did that moment she caught his eyes, the day before. Even though it couldn't have been more than a second or two, the look she gave, so hopeful and sincere melted the doctor's heart. By the next evening he had already arranged to take the night off and was pacing around is flat, waiting for time to leave.

After arguing with himself for days on end on whether not to attend, once the moment was upon him he felt like he would surely collapse if he didn't go right then and she was all to blame. Never mind that he loved music as much as the next man did. Music, in his opinion was what riveted the soul to the body. Tonight, however, he would have gladly given way to let that fettered spirit let loose and fly away, so long as it meant seeing her.

On a night like this, he almost believed it possible. The summer's evening that was opening night, flew in on the wings of a balmy breeze that was just perfect for a walk to the cathedral. He arrived just in time to see his fellow concert goers file in on either side of the towering sanctuary.

At first, upon entering the hall his presence seemed to go unnoticed by the crowd, allowing him to slip in fast and find his seat. Perhaps they were too busy, thinking about the young musician and the music ahead. Alternatively, perhaps that was just him. Either way, it did not last long much to his dismay. Before he could reach his seat it seemed all at once, the conversation came to a halt, sealing the world in a vacuum.

For a moment, he thought he would strangle in the silence as the people stared. Then, a rash of speculative whispers broke out like a pox amongst the crowd, causing him to draw in a steadying breath. You never knew how biting the word of your fellow man could be, until it was turned against you. With all the decorum and poise of one who had rubbed shoulders with far too many party members to be comfortable, he took his seat.

They need not know he was unnerved. He would show no sign of discomfort. Stiff-backed yet obviously relaxed he began reading the program, ignoring the fingers that pointed his way. Let them point. What harm could it do him? None, he supposed, even as he suppressed the urge to pull at his over tight collar. Was it perhaps a bit warm in here, or was it just him? Did the other viewers feel such discomfort as they took their seat? He didn't know and didn't have time to question it further as the lights dimmed suddenly.

Even the whisperings of the spectators died down to nothing as light music began to play. Then, from nowhere sprang the voice of a young man, who stood center stage, ostensibly having been born from the very air itself. Had he been so caught up in his own performance to have missed the young man take the stage? Perhaps, though it mattered not now. He was all eyes and ears as the song lead on, holding and sweeping him away to another world.

By the time it came down to the feature soloist, he had completely forgotten his reason for being there and for a moment was confused as to why Evelina was stepping out onto the stage. His heart quickened and breath stopped. He felt his mouth go dry. Then she opened her mouth and he felt as if he would sob from the beauty of it all. The sound that came was one of such pure, angelic beauty and power he felt his whole being shudder with physical shock.

Blind and dumb to all around him he sat, near weeping as the sound lifted him up and out of his corporeal form. The air was warm and fragrant, even as he unconsciously held his breath. His lungs burned, yet he did not notice. Then it happened. As clear as the face his eyes could not leave, he saw the answer to it all. Laid out before him, the vision carried him to the world of the future and his work. Success surrounded the methodology. Teachers from all over the world praised him. He had done it. This was it. This was the key to it all and from his elevated view on high; he could see exactly what he needed to do.

Suddenly, the music slowed. The crescendo had reached its peak and the concert was coming to a slow end. The moment passed and he felt as though he were sinking, lower and lower until he could feel the chair underneath his fingers, clutching the armrest for dear life. Suddenly, as if nothing had happened at all, he was himself again but what had brought him back he couldn't say. Then he realized. The music was over.

Dumbfounded and weak, he watched mutely the hall flooded with the sound of applause. People were standing up to clap while others whistled from their seats. The show was over. Now the sound of retreating feet echoed through the halls as the onlookers made their way to ostensibly more interesting ground. Gathering himself, he stood and followed the trooping flock out into another part of the large church where people were shaking hands with the performers. Everyone smiled and congratulated the singers for a job well done while he searched the crowd for one single face. There, amongst the largest group of admirers she stood, cornered on all sides. Everyone wanted a word with the beautiful young woman but none so much as the good doctor.

Standing on the outskirts of the small crowd, he could hear the people thanking her profoundly. One woman wept openly as she embraced her while several others cried silently. "You have the voice of an angel," he heard one man tell her while an old man shook her hand with tears in his withered eyes.

While he wanted to speak to her, he refused to ruin her shining moment. If they caught sight of the two of them, together it might cause a stir and he didn't want to include her in that. So he hung back, waiting. It must have been almost an hour before he managed to catch her eye through the crowd. Glancing casually over the shoulder of one of her admirers, he saw her start as if unaware he had been there. Then she smiled. That smile had her eyes light up like a beacon as she crossed the floor to meet him. His heart thundered in his chest as he watched what could only be described as pure elegance march across the open floor. He smiled.

"I am glad to see you could make it, Dr. Lozanov," her voice was formal for the benefit of those around them, even as the crowd was starting to thin out. It was late now and people wanted to be going home. In truth, he too should be making his way back so late at night, yet he stayed. A few hours of sleep wouldn't be missed.

"It would have been a travesty to miss it," He said quietly. More so than she could know, he realized as he offered her his arm. "Shall I walk you out, Miss Evelina?"

She nodded and he took her arm; he couldn't help but grin as his heart leaped to near soaring. If only he could articulate to her his gratitude as they stepped out, but the words failed him. There was so much he wanted to say. Would that prying eyes and ears were not hovering around so he could speak openly with her. Alas, he could not however on the chance that someone was around to overhear them. Finally, deciding it was best to say nothing at all, he chose his next topic of conversation. "Do you know your voice is the definition of perfection?" He asked simply, halting as they reached her car.

While some, when complemented, puffed up with pride and others might refute the claim with false modesty, she did neither. Instead, she just beamed at him, her cheeks flushed with pleasure even in the dim light of the evening. "Thank you," she said simply.

Was it the summer's breeze that played with a tendril of hair near her cheek, or just the stars reflected in her eyes? He couldn't say for sure but something struck him just then as she let go to unlock her little car that made him reach out. For only a moment, he held her tiny little hand in his, a million words on his mind. Then, someone nearby spoke and the moment was gone. Letting go, he turned to leave, but not before giving her hand a light squeeze with his own.

"No, thank you." He smiled, waving to her before turning toward his own vehicle.

* * * *

He met the next morning hours before the rest of the world. From the concert, he had gone straight home and began work. He hadn't even slept and more than likely wouldn't for several hours still. There was too much to be done today for any rest to be had.

In his work as a psychotherapist, he had discovered the power of suggestion. Over the years, he had learned that the human mind was capable of so many wondrous things, so long as one knew how to tap into one's resources. At first, in the early years he had worked heavily with hypnosis. He had been a young man, younger than he was now and just in his practice. People were already speaking very highly him and his work, even though he had not been a doctor very long.

Hypnosis was then and still thought to be a miracle for mental medical science and thought to do wonders. No one knew of the damages it could cause. He remembered well how he felt, after finally discovering the truth. It seemed to work well enough for his patients and he utilized it for a year or so before he realized that all was not as well as he would like. While yes, hypnosis could help heal the mind, to an extent, it could also harm if it was over used. At this point in his life and professional work, he usually advised against it all together unless strictly necessary. But it was not so, in the early days. Not until discovering what harm it could do to a person.

After that startling revelation, he had turned away from it completely. It had been hard, at the time seeing as how that had been a large part of how he handled his practice. What then, to do with his patients? That question plagued him for many hours back in those early days. There had even been a moment there where he had been convinced he was guilty of some horrible crime after realizing the hypnotic method could indeed be dangerous.

A new book had come into his possession at the hand of a friend, explaining the expense of change of character it could bring about in a person while weakening the will and depriving the person of initiative. This of course worried the young doctor, making him fear for his patients. Could he have harmed someone the whole time he thought he was helping? Could he have made things worse?

Guilt plagued him for days on end, leaving him both helpless and hopeless until, without a choice he ran to his dearest friend at the time, Brother Boyan. A wise, wonderful man and a teacher to people of all ages, the old man greeted him with the warm embrace of a father meeting a child upon seeing his upset. "Oh, come now Georgi," Brother Boyan smiled, clapping the young man on the shoulder. "Nothing is as bad as all that."

"Oh, but it is," The young Dr. Lozanov practically wailed as they walked. "I've committed and awful, horrible crime," he continued. They stopped. Brother Boyan looked at him quizzically.

"Have you killed a person?" The man asked. Distraught, Dr. Lozanov shook head and proceeded to explain his problem, heart heavy with shame. By the end of it, Brother Boyan was smiling.

"You did nothing wrong my young friend. You used your knowledge for medical purposes with the intention of doing good. There is no fault here. You just learn from it, and move on. You must be calm, my young friend. Always calm, for there is always something more to learn."

So there was that. Not only had the man been a good source of advice, from one doctor to another but a sort of father figure as well. In fact, the young doctor had admired the man so much that he had named his young son after him.

Even reassured that he was not some sort of horrible monster; he was still in quite a situation. What to do about his practice? After using hypnosis for so long, he wasn't sure what to do without it.

Up the entire night, he had been terrified to go to work that day. Even worse still to find another doctor waiting for him outside his office. A specialist in internal diseases, the man was to be observing him that day. Of all days. Not that it came as too much of a surprise since he was supposed to be teaching psychotherapy to his colleagues but oh! Of all the days to ask.

His first inclination was to refuse and feign sudden illness. Considering the cold sweat that crept down his back, it might have been true! However, he did not want to lie and he certainly did not want to leave and risk missing someone who was ill. Nevertheless, how could it be helped? What would he do if someone did need him? Everything he had known to work so well, the core of his practice, had been ruined. He could not risk endangering someone for the sake of saving face. No. That would never do.

He would just have to turn the man down today and as him to come back at another time. Steeling himself to do exactly that, he opened his mouth to speak just as a light tap echoed through the little door that closed his office off to the rest of the institute. His heart dropped to the floor below.

Tentatively, as though a monster stood waiting on the other side, he answered the knock, opening the door slowly. There he saw a round, red-faced woman with sad eyes and a tired looking face. Those eyes, so loud in their plea for help called to him and he felt his heart sink. Stepping aside, he let her in, resigning himself to his fate. He would have to improvise, he supposed and sat himself down to listen.

While the woman was not actually ill, it was not hard to see she needed help, though after a moment of listening to her, he realized he was not actually needed. For an hour or more he sat, listening without interruption. As the woman talked on about her life, her children, her husband, and all the accompanying problems thereafter. All he had to do was nod and give a sympathetic frown now and again. Once she was finished and he had heard the story through he nodded and thanked her profoundly.

"Thank you very much," he said genuinely, smiling at the lady. "Thank you very much. Come tomorrow again!" And she left. The rest of the day was carried on without incident and he made his way home.

The next day, the other doctor was there again and without fail, so was the woman from the day before.

"Dr. Lozanov, what did you do?" Her face seemed several years younger to him now as she smiled delightedly at the two of them. "I am well! I thank you very much!"

Excited and smiling the woman left, so enthusiastically in fact she forgot to close the door. Standing to correct her over sight, Dr. Lozanov was unsurprised to see his college looking at him, obviously quite puzzled.

"Really, what did you do to her?" he asked.

Smiling more to himself than anyone else, Georgi shrugged. "I know how to listen, my colleague." He answered, hearing the truth of it even as he realized it himself. "When I listen to the patient, he or she sees that I listen to them with understanding."

It made sense well enough. Something in his face, perhaps. Maybe it was just his overall demeanor. Whatever it was he knew it was not limited to him alone. Perhaps if others could listen so well? After all, in truth that was the only thing the woman had needed.

Others as well. While yes, now and again some came to him that needed medical attention and were actually ill, most of them only needed his ears. Others came to watch and learn from him. He always made certain that in demonstrating, it was clear what the attitude toward the patient was. Not commanding or insisting. Not enslaving so to say but a gentle communication from one person to the next.

It was then he began to truly learn that it was not necessary to talk a lot in his work. To listen though, that was the key. To love the person who was in front of him and to be certain they knew he loved them, for them to *feel* it. To listen to the patient with an attitude of caring concern for their life, their health, their needs. It was that he realized that had influenced the woman a hundred times more than any other method he could have used.

This was what he explained to each of his colleagues, who were amazed that someone could understand these concepts and put them to practice.

From there it was not so difficult to come to his main work, suggestopedia.

Chapter 9

While it was not a difficult conclusion to come to, the creation of the methodology was still a gradual process and had been since the beginning. Unlike what many of his rather unsavory colleges seemed to think, he didn't just dream it up all in a day. Over time, through many experiments and exercises, it became clear to Georgi that the human memory was capable of so much more than originally given credit. Everything in the memory remained as it was first taken in. One only needed to know the right way to tap into and use the vast resources that was the reserve capacity.

However, how to prove this? And what exactly was that 'right' way. He has certainly seen some of the wrong ways, in his years as a doctor. In fact, for a short time there he had been guilty of that wrong way himself, when thinking such things as hypnosis could cure all. Quick to discover the damaging effects of such practices in excess he had turned away from them, never to look back.

But that had been a long time ago and thinking about the past was certainly not going to get anything done.

"Would that it did," he sighed to himself, combing over more papers. Yes indeed, would that thinking over times long gone *could* yield more answers, but alas. It did not and that meant that he was stuck looking over old case files until he got a better idea.

What frustrated him the most was the feeling that he was *so* close, and yet, here he was so frustrated.

Surely, there was an answer. He knew his work was made of sterner stuff than this, to be knocked down by a stalemate. There was too much work behind it, to allow that.

Years of research, clinical cases and inside studies as well as some experiments helped to prove the theory. More often than not, the idea proved itself, without much direction from him at all. Like the instance with Dushko, a psychotherapy patient for who used to come in the evenings, when he had just opened his practice. Many of his patients had served as living examples of his methods and were the better for it but none so much as this young man. Even then, all those years ago it was plain to the doctor that he was onto something. But what and how to prove it? That was the question.

A question that had been answered almost easily, one evening after a session with the young man. Throughout their time together that evening, Dr. Lozanov couldn't help but notice how agitated the young man seemed to be. Fidgeting, absentminded and hardly able to concentrate, the boy was a mess.

"Is there something troubling you?" He asked the boy just as he was leaving for the day. Stopping at the door, the young man turned and looked at up at Georgi with an almost pained expression.

"Doctor, I am going now to the evening school but…I am very afraid." The young man paused to swallow, his face slightly pale. "We are to recite our poems tonight and I have not learned one poem by heart. I do not know it and I do not know what to do."

Ah. Therefore, that was the problem. A bad mark in the book could be detrimental to a young person these days. If he were to have a bad mark today, it would follow him for the rest of his life. With an understanding frown, the doctor thought quickly over his studies over the last few months. Could now be the time to see if he was right? If, on the chance he was incorrect, it wouldn't hurt the lad any more than having nothing at all would have…but if he was right, it could save the day. Dare he? The question weighed heavily on the doctors mind for a long, long moment.

"Dushko, have you heard the poem at least once?"

Nodding slowly the boy ran his hands through his hair. "Yes, the teacher read it to us the day before."

Nodding himself in a determined sort of way, Georgi approached the boy in a confident manner. "The answer to your problem is simple enough." He told him, knowing it was true without a doubt. "If you have heard it, it is in your subconscious," he began, opening the door to the office. "Then you know it." He led him out, one arm around his shoulder in a friendly, reassuring way. "You must be calm and everything will be alright." He smiled. "When they ask you, catch the first word which comes to your mind and say the whole poem. It is simple as that. Do not say you do not know it, or that you have not studied."

Still smiling strong and confident, he lead the boy on, each falling into step with the other as they walked and talked. "You must believe what I say is true or they will put a poor mark on your book. You do not want this." At that, he let the young man go, stepping back just as they reached the outside door. That was that. He watched his patient take an audible breath and then wave goodbye as he went about his way. The rest of the evening for him was spent in excited anticipation as he wondered how his young friend was doing. Thankfully, he did not have to wait too terribly long to find out.

The next evening he arrived on time as always, but with an excitement to his face Dr. Lozanov had rarely seen before. "Doctor, what do you think has happened? They asked me for the poem and I remembered what you told me. I caught the first word and said the whole poem without mistake!" Holding up his grade book the young man practically bounce in place with jubilant triumph. "You see?"

After that, it was obvious to the doctor that his theory was correct. That almost all was kept in the subconscious and one simply needed the knowledge to activate it. From there, it was a small step to mull over how such knowledge could be used in the practice. Of course, there were other cases. Some postgraduate studies in brain physiology at the Bulgarian Academy of Science were taken. More studies done to further the theory and of course everything was documented. But how to utilize it all? This question had plagued him for so long, up until now. Thanks to Evelina and her concert, he now knew. Music. Music was the key to everything. After all, it all made sense did it not? How often did you see something learned faster once put into music instead of just by itself?

Of course, the methodology would have to be reworked a bit here and there but that should not be so much of a problem.

There was his struggle. After working through the night after the concert, pouring through his combined work from the last several years, he found some music of the classical art that seemed like it would work well. For a while, at least. But it still left something…*lacking.* He needed something more. For now, to some extent, the classical music could be used but he knew he needed music written specifically for the Suggestology.

A few gentle experiments showed better results than he had had in months. But it could be better! He knew it could. Meaning that he needed music written for the work. This however did bring him to a problem. He was a doctor, not a musician. Even if he had some knowledge of music theory, it was plain to see that it would take more than a hopeful amateur to serve his needs.

He needed a professional. But how to find one? Of course, Evelina, the herald of his great epiphany, was the first to spring to mind. She would be finished with her other course soon so maybe... No. Not now. With so much else in her life, her divorce, her mother , her new job which she seemed to be doing so well at...no, he would not ask her. Better hire someone who could devote their time to it than ask such a busy woman. After coming to this conclusion, he made a decision.

An advertisement was placed in the local paper. The institute needed professional musicians for research. It seemed simple enough to him and he expected an influx of volunteers yet day after day went by without word. Had he been mistaken? A whole week passed without even a hint of response. Then, finally on the eighth day, a man applied. A violinist no less, which seemed a good sign to Georgi.

Grey eyed and nice enough at first the man seemed a bit... withdrawn to Dr. Lozanov's eyes, though he shrugged off the initial judgment. He had worked with people far too long to let shyness steer him away. Especially now in his time of need. After explaining his wants and needs in simple terms, the next thing to do of course was see him play. After all, no point in taking the man on if he was not worth his salt.

Without much formality or presentation, they began, him settling down to listen while the grey-eyed man began his piece. The first few notes wheezed out from the strings like a death rattle, setting Georgi on edge instantly. Before the song was a full breath length long, he knew that this would never work. Was it only him?

As others began to gather around, patient and doctor alike at the open door, he watched their faces carefully. Did they wince and recoil at the sound? Did they shudder or pale as the macabre melody sliced through the once dulcet afternoon? No, to his shock they did not. In fact, they seem to enjoy it and even clapped as the violinist paused, his first song now completed. Watching from behind the desk, Georgi felt the color drain from his cheeks as empty eyes looked at him, as though waiting for encouragement.

It..wasn't so much that he was bad. In fact, he was quite technically good. However…there was something missing. Despite a near standing ovation from the gathering crowd of onlookers, the man simply did not set well with the doctor. Not only did they not seem to mesh well as people, but also his ideas were too much a different vision than the doctor wanted. Too far away from what the work needed.

Should he let him play again? Did he really want to hear anymore? While he doubted it very much, he nodded none the less, eternally wincing even as he did so.

Who was this…this coarse, empty man? Not so much in attitude, but in spirit the man seemed almost like a ghost. His eyes reflected nothing and as he played Dr. Lozanov felt almost sick to his stomach. It should be plain to anyone that there was something seriously lacking, even if not in the music than at least the man. He was not a bad man and not a bad person. But there was just something wrong. But then why did the onlookers cheer? Was it only him? On the surface, the violinist was a technical wonder, each note executed perfectly. Without hesitation or fault, the demonstration was perfect, save one thing. A lack of life. No matter how hard he exerted himself to listen and hear the music, Georgi was constantly aware of that one missing component.

It was like the sound a haunted spirit, whisked away and forgotten in the arms of death, but still unwillingly tied to the earth. Even after the session was over, the stinging vibrations hung in the air like a half-ghost of what *could* have been a spectacular performance. Was it only him? No one else seemed to notice the chill that had settled over the room, or the presence of a hundred little ghosts settled in their gut. Perhaps it was just him?

He thought about the possibility as they talked about the methodology. Even had he not been so uncomfortable, it was quite clear that this particular partnership would never work. Their ideas were too different ideas. Too far removed from each other and going in completely wrong direction. It was an uncomfortable feeling thinking about the ideas of the young man and his attitude toward the work. The thing that stood out was complete the lack of love or spirit the man displayed. It was a job to him, nothing more.

How could a man play so well and yet, it made him almost sick to hear it? Where was the *life* in the sound? Where was the love? To his ears, he could hear none. Never the less, Dr. Lozanov tried to put his ill feelings aside, giving the man the benefit of the doubt over several days' worth of sessions. Word spread amongst the practice. Could this be it? They all wondered if the young man would become a permanent fixture to the practice. All but Dr. Lozanov. Try as he might, he just could not shake the unease he felt with the man.

So, left without much choice, he did the only thing he knew: dismissed him. Of course, some kind of perfunctory politeness was put forward, explaining away any question as to why he was not right for the work. While he did not like the man, and certainly did not like the music, he could not find the heart to tell him so, or be unkind toward him. He had no problem with him as an individual, but in the workplace, there was no room for him. Perhaps, in some cases, it was better to bend the truth and spare the soul that tell the truth and kill the man with your honesty.

"I certainly hope so," he mumbled to himself, running his fingers through his hair with a sigh. The day was lost. Spent and mishandled on the glass man and his music and now he had no idea what to do. Disappointed beyond reason he began rummaging through his texts and various papers as though hoping an answer would fall into his lap.

CHAPTER 10

§。

Two weeks had passed since the man with the violin had come into his office. As day by day crawled by at the pace of a snail and still no other solutions came, he wondered if he had been hasty in dismissing the young musician. Even so, he just could not bring himself to call him back. There would have to be another option, he just knew it. After trying various pieces of classical work and seeing some progress, he could tell he was on the right track. The only problem was the music. Any common piece could help, certainly, but this work demanded more than just the common. It needed its own music, something he could not provide without a musician's help. That left him with quite a situation, one which he would not find an answer to until at least a week or two later.

Late one night after a long afternoon, he was done for the day and just about to leave. Almost the moment the clock struck 11:00 pm and he was lifting his briefcase from the floor there was a knock at the door. Surprised to be called upon so late he turned to frown at the sound, wondering.

"Who could it be, at this hour," he mumbled to himself before calling a loud welcome. "Yes, come in!" His voice was confident though almost weary at the same time. Sudden joy colored his face as he watched the late night visitor push the door handle down and step in, smiling. "Evelina! What are you doing here at that time of the evening?" Bright green eyes were looking at her in amusement as a sudden surge of pleasure rushed through him.

What a picture she was, standing on the threshold to his office. Brown hair fell freely to her shoulders as her eyes were sparkled brightly in the dim light. It was strange, even in the company of one he considered a friend to realize he had been subconsciously reading her body language, as he would have a patient.

Cues he might have missed otherwise told the tale of a young woman who was nervous, despite her vivid smile. Her back was drawn tight, her breath uncertain and a little faster than it should have and from the corner of his eye, he could see her fingers twitching absently. Could something be wrong? From the look on her face, he doubted it and yet, she seemed tense somehow but before he could even ask, she was taking a breath to speak.

"Dr. Lozanov, I...I have come to tell you that you need me." She almost whispered. Feeling his eyebrows fly up into his greying hairline as he gaped at her, more than slightly taken aback. For a moment, he stayed like that until he realized he more than likely looked just a little ridiculous, just then. Snapping his mouth shut with a click, he shook his head a little.

"Evelina, I..." He began, obviously a little a lost for words.

It struck him just then at the way her usually easy shoulders seemed to be squared, as though she was determined. What was he missing? What exactly was this all about? He wondered as she looked him in the face, fixing his gaze to hers as she handed him a neatly folded piece of paper. Unfolding it, he still looked at her, unflinching until the moment he looked down to read what seemed to be... a newspaper clipping? The black and white ink was stark in the yellow lighting of his desk lamp as he bent over the desk to better read it.

A news clipping indeed, with the usual cheap print and tiny letters that made a person squint just to read the thing. This however he had no trouble reading as his eyes scanned the cut out with fervor, landing almost instantly on his own want ad. "Institution announces competition for musicians in the name of science," the lettering read, circled in red ink with one long swipe of the red pen he knew she always carried with her. The announcement had been placed in the paper not all that long ago, but so far, he had had no one but the young man. Did this mean what he thought it did?

"Evelina…I…" He started, only to have her cut him off.

"When do you want me to begin?"

As soon as possible of course was the answer and so they did, diving into the work almost instantly. With the course she had been taking over and done with, they both decided it would be best if she participated in his course at the institute. That way they could work together easily while she learned about the program.

With her by his side and the two of them working together he found his work blossomed into something else altogether. In the two weeks he had been waiting on an answer, he had already implemented classical music into the study process. Now that she was there, she was already working on a program written specifically for the work. Music to be played specifically for each moment, for each session was being planned out and written according to the suggestopedic process of instruction.

While only a student of the work at the moment, she showed intuition far beyond that of a pupil and was often able to guess what the next step of the process would be. With such sincere interest, it was easy enough for him to see he had made the right decision. It was also easy for him to realize that he was falling in love with her. How could he not?

With every day that they met, he felt his heart swell at the sight of her a little more. From early morning to sometimes-late evening, though he tried not to keep her late very often, they were together.

Now and again, it would occur to him to wonder what she must think him and wondered if those glances of hers were just a bit more than inquisitive. Perhaps she held his eyes just a moment too long or maybe, her hand lingered on his for just a second, when passing papers or the like back and forth. In fact, he would have left it be, were it not for her.

Well, at least, he had have left it be a little longer. Not too long. After all, surely he wasn't noticed that while totally professional at work, outside of work their conversation was just a bit lighter… perhaps more playful? Then again, there were always the moments late at night, when they would leave the work be for the evening and just talk. Of everything, it seemed. The deep concerns of the soul, the longing of the human heart. It was one evening such as that, which put it all into perspective for him, in fact.

"You know," he said to her one evening, his voice casual. Dare he ask? "You tell me often what you think people want, but, how is it you know?" Stacking a bundle of random papers on his desk, he made careful eye contact with curious orbs that glanced back at him, grey depths glittering.

"I know what the ears want," she told him simply, shrugging as though it was the simplest of questions. "If you listen to what the ears want, you learn what the heart wants."

"Really now?" Dr. Lozanov smiled warmly, charmed by the idea. "But what of the musician?" His smile was somewhat teasing now. "What is it you want? Would you tell me?" Folding his hands across the desk, he wondered if she would share herself like this with him, tell him something so personal.

"Well…" As she bit her lip now, he watched her think for a moment as if deciding something. What the decision of that internal conflict was, he never knew. What, if anything he knew about the word was forgotten as a tiny hand rested itself on his own, for just a moment.

"Perhaps I hope my heart speaks for itself, through my music if not my words." She told him quietly, smiling. Then as if to break his hold, she pulled away. What happened next, well, one might have said it was poor impulse control? Another could have argued it was simply a few years' worth of karmic attraction, finally built to prime. Either way, he couldn't say. He only knew that to have her pull away in just that moment was the last thing he wanted and pulled her hand back gently, but firmly.

"And what would it tell me, if it did?" His voice a whisper, as he asked almost desperately.

For a long moment she simply looked at him and he at her, hands clasped just so.

He watched with a pounding heart as a slow smile spread across her face. "It would tell you a lot of things, if you have the time to listen…"

It was his turn to smile as he linked his fingers with hers across the desk. "If you would be willing to tell me, I have all the time in the world."

CHAPTER 11

The few months of study and work paid off well for Evelina. Before she knew it, she was already finished with her German course and signing up for Dr. Lozanov's. It seemed appropriate that if she was to help him, she have a better understanding of the methodology and its workings. Not to mention, it also allowed her to see the good doctor quite often, something the both enjoyed, though at times she had to wonder if she enjoyed it a bit more. Not that she had bothered to ask…The subject of her feelings for him were a complex and delicate matter, one which she would have hesitated to mention even under the best of circumstances, much less just shortly after both their divorces.

That reasoning however didn't stop her from wishing things were different. Whether passing him in the hallway or simply hearing his name mentioned outside of school hours, the radiant glow that lit her face was plain to anyone who saw her.

"You're looking lovely today, Evelina," one of her friends remarked upon seeing her in the hall of the university, echoing similar words she had heard all week long. She was used to it by now and simply nodded and murmured a quiet thank you, all the while comforted by the little secret that sat snuggled in her chest. Being in love again was a wonderful feeling and it carried her throughout the day with a light in her eyes and a smile on her face. She would remain that way for the next several months, up to and well passed the completion of Dr. Lozanov's course and well beyond, when it was decided she could start working at the institute.

It was not all smiles however, once she found herself inserted into the daily workings of the staff. It was never anything overt, but she got the feeling now and again that some members didn't approve of her being there. Especially not the females working closest to Dr. Lozanov who suddenly found themselves second priority. Of course, staff members had sisters and daughters and cousins they'd all like to introduce the doctor to, but it seemed a fruitless endeavor. A person would have been blind to see that he had eyes for no other than her.

She tried not to let it get to her, and with the doctor behind her, most days she just let it roll right off her back, without notice. Occasionally however, she would hear something every now and again that would make her think better about what she was doing.

"She doesn't even have a formal education." One female coworker hissed to another in the middle of lunch break, about two months after Evelina had begun her work at the office. Just loudly enough for Evelina to hear her over the noise of everything else. While they didn't dare let the good doctor know of their disapproval of his star partner, they certainly didn't mind flaunting it in front of her.

"I wonder what on earth he sees in her." The other remarked over her tea. What indeed. That was a good question. At least, to others it must be. She knew her abilities well and didn't doubt them for a moment. But without the formal degree to prove it, others might have to wonder.

It seemed to her that to better assist her beloved doctor and to better complete her work, a formal university degree must be procured. Until now, she thought it more than unnecessary. She could have and probably should have had one before now, at least in music, though until now, she saw it as pointless.

Her music was no better for some bit of paper to hang on her wall and neither was her voice. However, if it meant being able to further what she could do for both herself and her beloved doctor, then perhaps it was the best course. Not to mention her *teaching* could certainly benefit from it as well and if nothing else, it would at least give her supposed colleagues less to speculate about, if not earn their respect out right. However, if she were to be honest with herself, their respect was the least of her concern. Her beloved, brilliant doctor on the other hand was a completely different story. She wanted to help him as much as possible and to do that, it seemed she would have to get her degree. It seemed the most logical course to her.

Therefore, with that enlightening conversation in mind, she decided when and how she planned to do everything. Fitting everything into her schedule, which she carefully worked out with Georgi, it was decided within a matter of days. She would begin the study for a BA in Italian Philology at the University of Sofia. That, coupled with beginning the work on two separate projects for the institute had her with enough to do for several months. Even with all of that going on, she was still able to dream up and bring to life not one, but two separate suggestopedic operas for children, plus a book just recently started. It did not leave her much time for much of anything other than work and sleep but she did not mind. Her boy was well settled and spending most of his time at school of course and with his father on the weekends. They both seemed perfectly happy about it and so was she.

In fact, she was ecstatic to see them bonding so well with one another and happy that they could. After the divorce, she had wondered how they might do with one another and it had made her nervous but overall, they seemed to get along better now than they had before. That left her with plenty of time on her hands to work without worrying whether or not her sweet boy was happy when she was not around, even if it left them little time to spend with each other. But it was all right. As always, she relished the challenge.

She also enjoyed the time she spent with Georgi, which was quite often, now that they were working together and he was helping her to study and brush up for various exams and technical explanations of music theory and whatever else she was doing at the time. She never noticed. The textbooks were nearly untouched for most of the study period, unnoticed as she sailed through class after class with flying colors.

It all went by rather quickly.

Day in, day out they worked together no matter what the objective. Even the most deplorable task was made just a little better, when he was helping her and it was lovely to spend so much time together. Then again, it also made her worry for him, now that she was seeing more of him. Until now, she had never realized how tired he must be all the time but now that they were working so closely, it was hard not to notice. Despite the tireless face he tried to present to the world, once the staff was gone and everything closed for the day, that mask came down.

She often saw through it regardless, but there was never so much of a shock until the end of the day when he could no longer hide the exhaustion. Inevitably, she would end up trying to convince him to go home to rest almost every other evening. Of course, he turned her down every time. Regardless of weekends or holidays, he was always there before sunrise and long passed sunset. It was one of the things she loved about him, his unwavering devotion. When the last staff member was gone for the night, she was still there, staying as late as he did.

With him as a shining example, it was easy for her to want much the same. To strive to further herself and her passions for the better of others as well as herself. From early morning, before the rest of the world had even stirred, she was there, waiting to begin the day. Not even a month into the process and they had doubled their efforts two fold. Time flew like a shot, baffling him as six months slipped away into absolutely nothing. In truth, it was hard for him not to wonder how he had ever managed to get along without her. At anything he asked her to do, she aimed to do it perfectly.

It was plain to see she devoted every ounce of her living soul to see that it was done as best as it could be. Even the most simple of tasks were made to be top priority in her eyes. Without arrogance or pride, she composed wonders, astounding him and all her music touched with the beauty of it all. With a profound thinking and deep, thorough understanding, she was the perfect partner. As much as he could, he tried to see that they were constantly together, both in and out of work. Whether a late night conference for discussion over the textbooks they were starting to write, or just simple dinner date, he tried to make sure they saw each other at least once a day.

It was a dinner date on a late Friday evening that had her practically dancing as they met that evening.

"What a face," he told her, eyes laughing as they embraced one another. "What has you so happy this evening?"

What indeed was the news that the Sofia opera house had contacted her earlier that evening, offering up their best performers for "The Land of Children" just recently completed?

"Oh but that is wonderful!" He exclaimed after she had finished explaining. It made her heart swell to see him so happy. She didn't even notice her food as it was served. All she could see was the glowing individual who sat in front of her, avidly outlining the next stage of the textbooks in between bites of pasta. Did it get any better than this? She wondered as she picked over her own plate.

Their work was esteemed in both fields of music and mental health and even beyond. Teachers had begun contacting them, asking for more information. A group of 10th grade students chosen at random from Sofia was taking classes at the Institute of Suggestology, learning all subjects suggestopedically. So far, they showed better marks across the board than even the best of their peers after only a few short weeks. That, and agreement between the governments of Austria and the People's Republic Bulgaria had begun a recent experiment in the Pedagogical Academy of Vienna! Of course, there was tension now and again.

Just the other day someone appointed by the Ministry of Education and Ministry of Health had come to observe them, checked both the acquisition of the material and the health of the children. This was one of many specialists and scientists to visit but so far, the conclusions were always positive. In a few days there was to be the first international conference on the question of Suggestology, to take place in the House of the Scientists, from 5 until 10.

This was something they were both extremely nervous over, but she had a feeling it would go well. How could it not? Whether faith in the man, faith in the work or a little of both, she could not say but beyond any doubt, she knew it would be well. How could not be?

"It will be alright, won't it?" She asked, folding her hands in front of herself on the table once their plates had been taken away. The smile he gave her made her wonder why she'd even asked at all, despite the lingering doubt that soured her chest.

"Of course it will," he said softly, taking one of her tiny hands and holding it with his own. "How can it now be? With you by my side, everything will always be alright."

CHAPTER 12

❧

The days leading up to the meeting crawled by at the pace of a snail. Everything from work to everyday, mundane activities changed, hampered by the tension that plagued them both. Even with the air practically sparking with suspense at every turn, they somehow managed to stay relatively calm. It was a near thing, especially with surprises popping up here there and everywhere, including one Dr. Lozanov had never expected.

It was a rainy day, around noon when the man turned up at his door. Evelina was out running an errand to the opera house to speak with the director about an upcoming presentation and everyone else was taking their lunch. The office was empty, except for Georgi when there was a knock at the door. "Come in!" He called merrily over his shoulder, as his hands were full of books and the sandwich he had brought for his own noon meal.

The door creaked open with its usual screech that was almost accepted at this point and was unnoticed by the doctor. What was a surprise however was the sound of a rather familiar voice behind him.

"It's good to see you again, Dr. Lozanov." The man said quietly. Dr. Lozanov turned and stood up from where he had bent to reach a lower bookshelf and was surprised to come face to face with Georgi Gateva, Evelina's ex-husband whom he recognized from his many visits to the house, when Evelina's mother had still been alive. Almost every time he had been stinking drunk and sullen, barely saying a word to the doctor outside of the usual pleasantries, and that was on a good day. Most of the time, he had ignored him and the goings on in his home, as long as everyone was quiet. Today however, he seemed perfectly sober and greeted the doctor with a firm handshake, once Lozanov had a free hand to offer.

"It's…good to see you too, Mr. Gateva." The doctor replied, somewhat at a loss for words. Of all the people to show up at his door, the tall engineer was certainly the last person he thought he'd see. "Can I help you with something?" He asked. "Here," gesturing toward, the doctor smiled. "Have a seat."

While somewhat taken aback by the man's sudden appearance, Dr. Lozanov certainly wasn't going to be rude. If he had come here, then he must need some sort of help with something and Dr. Lozanov planned to do everything he could to help, just as he would anyone else.

Once he was seated, Dr. Lozanov smiled. "Can I offer you some water or a cup of coffee?" He offered. Mr. Gateva shook his head. Apparently, today it was all business.

"I have come to speak with you about Evelina, actually." He said as the doctor took his own chair.

"No, no," he laughed at the sudden look on Dr. Lozanov's face. "I have only come to ask you to take good care of her." He smiled now, almost sadly. "I know that we are no longer together, which I think is better for both of us and I know I should have treated her better, when we were."

The man shrugged now. "But I did not. That is in the past now. The only thing I can do is come to you to make sure her future is better and to say please take care of her."

Dr. Lozanov smiled, eyes reflecting sudden warmth that was almost tangible. "I doubt I could do anything else." Never mind that he and the young singer were not together, or that he had even told her of his feelings. She might not know, but the rest of the world certainly seemed to and treated the couple as an item wherever they went. It was no surprise to Dr. Lozanov that the singer's former husband had heard about it. In fact, the only thing that surprised him was that he had not heard about it until now. That and his presence in the office that day.

"Good man," the engineer smiled and clapped the doctor on the shoulder in a friendly sort of manner. Even if the smile didn't quite meet his eyes, Lozanov knew he meant it. How must it be for this man to have been married to her for so many years, than see her go to someone else after the marriage had crumbled? Worse yet, put your pride aside and go and ask that someone else to take care of her in his stead? He couldn't imagine what pain the man must be in, even though he didn't show it.

"Are you sure you will not take that cup of coffee?" Dr. Lozanov offered gently as the man stood to leave. The engineer shook his head. They shook hands again, silently before the man left and Dr. Lozanov was alone again, left to think over the odd occurrence of what had just transpired between the two men. By the time Evelina returned, he was still sitting in the same place, nursing a cup of cold coffee that sat beside his forgotten sandwich.

"Are you alright?" She asked him quietly, laying her hand over his knuckles were they sat white from holding the cup too long.

"Hmmm?" He looked up, absentmindedly, eyes almost vapid until they caught hers. "I'm fine." He smiled, bringing the other hand to rest atop hers. "I am perfectly fine."

And he was. The good mood carried him through the remaining days, tall and strong up until the big moment was upon them. Then he began to feel himself wilt a little from nervousness.

The conference was here, looming over the horizon like an overcast sky. They rushed through the morning, organizing last minute papers while rushing about, making sure nothing had been forgotten. With perhaps an hour's worth of sleep between them and a long road ahead, it was a wonder they managed to get everything together in one piece. By the time they actually made arrived at the resort, Evelina was surprised her beloved Georgi had any hair left. "Are you ready?" She whispered as she waited for the group to settle in and take their places.

"As ready as I will ever be I suppose." He replied with a long, nervous sigh. His heart thundered in his chest like a bird caught in a cage.

"Smile," she whispered encouragingly, just as their names were called.

With scientists from 13 countries from Europe and America, 7 main reports, 53 announcements from several major officials, it was a lot to take in as they were introduced and announced to the room at large. Several people clapped at the introduction while others simply sat speculatively, waiting. The interest was enormous; even more so than they could have guessed and she smiled just to feel him draw himself up strongly beside her.

It was his pride coming into play that held his shoulders with all the dignity of a professional in his element. As chairman of the institute, he had a duty to his colleagues, his students, and his patients to do his best and she knew beyond any doubt he would. He had not worked this hard for this long to fail now.

As usual, he did not disappoint. The organizing committee consisted of the scientific council of the Research Institute of Suggestology. Chairperson of honor, academician Sava Ganovski, was also there. Members of the governing body of the Bulgarian Academy of Science, head of the Psychological and Philosophical society of the People's Republic of Bulgaria plus several others.

It staggered the mind to see all the intellectuals of her country, gathered around to avidly discuss the work. Even as nervous as she had been, it melted away as soon as she found her seat. Her role was only to observe of course, but she did not try to hide the smile as she watched him deliver their case perfectly. The speech was well written in the firm but gentle manner that spoke of confidence in the work as well as the person, without having to be forceful.

With all experiments having been documented, not to mention the reports from all the officials come to observe them over the past few months, with 13 reports total, all of which positive and everything laid out on the table, there was not much he had to say. The work spoke for itself. People flooded him with questions of all kinds, without pause. He answered each one easily, as if he did this every day. No matter what the topic, he was able to hold himself upwards with the strength of a man who knew what he was doing.

Everyone was impressed and in no time at all, the business was concluded. It was time to go. After a short moment to collect the contact information of several people of interest, each one champing at the bit just to have a word with him, the pair excused themselves with smiles on their faces and a kick in their step that had not been there before. It was a very, very good day and neither of them could be happier.

Weeks of waiting and everything was finished in a matter of hours and carefully executed explanations. From everything they could gather they had been very well received despite the initial skepticism. Even better was to see the fruits of their labors harvested in the form of a contract for the application of suggestopedic methodology in the USA as well as several others, all thanks to the big interest generated by the conference. It was a wonderful day for Suggestology and for the two of them. A celebration was suggested, if nothing more than a simple dinner but in light of the recent success they decided the best celebration would be to get back to work.

"I couldn't eat anything right now if I tried," Evelina smiled excitedly. "We have far too much to do!" And indeed, they did. With the US, among others showing so much interest, they had several things to do in the next few weeks just to catch up with the high demand.

"Isn't it exciting?" He laughed as they made their way home. Indeed it was. Even rushing around, busy and tired all the time, neither one could have happier. They were on their way to what they were both reaching for, a shared dream between the two of them that was turning into reality as every second passed them by. All they had to do was keep up! For a moment, even with the conference standing behind them as a mark of victory in the growing distance she felt just a bit of fear. Could they really do this? Could she really devote herself to this dream?

Looking at him for a moment, she smiled to see him lit up by the setting sun. Perhaps this was the meaning if it all, she realized. Feeling her heart squeeze. Books romanticized the idyllic scene of the two lovers, staring into each other's with the look of longing after the triumph of the day. For many years, she herself thought she wanted much the same. Now, she thought different. Perhaps the meaning of it all was not to stare longingly into each other's eyes, but to look off toward the same direction, together, each sharing the others dream. The thought made her smile. It only lasted for a moment however, like a little brush against her confidence or a little tap on the shoulder before it was gone.

CHAPTER 13

§🍂

Seven Years later.

"How long has it been?" She gaped at him from across the shared workstation piled high with it's many books and papers. Could it have really been that long? "Seven years?" The answering nod she received was slow, though enthusiastic. Gentle sunlight poured through the immaculate office windows, surrounding the two of them in golden warmth. It was a lovely day in the city of Sofia, but even as perfect as it was, the sunlight couldn't seem to lighten up the dark that shadowed both their eyes with dread. The foreboding feeling had been with them for weeks now.

"Seven years." Georgi smiled. "Seven years since that conference and how many since then?" A dozen at least, that she could count. There might have even been a few that she had overlooked in the rush of everyday life. It was a rhetorical question anyway, which they both knew well. Their success was not measured by how many fruitful conferences they had had in the run so far, but how many people they had reached as a whole. Over time, she had become very satisfied with her role in things. Even after so many years, it never got old. As fast paced life at the institute was, it wasn't really a surprise to think about it. Not really.

"Think about all we've accomplished," the doctor sighed as she smiled. Seven years was a very long time even though it had all seemed to pass by in a blink. From Tokyo to Prague, Vienna and France they had been all over the world, to see and do and speak with many important people. Everywhere they went, the people greeted them with smiles and open arms. Several well received books had been written by both of them, over time as well as the children's operas and various musical pieces for the work. Not to mention two separate degrees earned by Dr. Evelina. Now she was giving her own lectures, as well as publishing her works that were viewed and respected just as highly as Dr. Lozanov's. They were, and had been since the beginning, partners in all things to each other. Now, it was the rest of the world that viewed them that was as well.

Yes, throughout the years they had done quite well together, despite disapproval in and out of the institute and if they weren't giving him flack about his choice of partner for his work, then they were staring down their noses at the closeness of their relationship. Even though they were of course nothing but professional inside the office, it had still been hard. In a small place where everyone knew your name it was unavoidable.

And despite all that, they were still strong. "Seven years since the first meeting and now another." He frowned at her now. To see that brilliant smile wilt into a drooping frown was a strange, unexpected sight. Had she not known better, her first reaction would have been to ask him what was wrong. There was no point in it today, however because it was the same thing that had her smile dissolving into nothing seconds at a time. The same thing that had been bothering them both for days. It hurt her to see him so worried but it was also unavoidable.

They both had had a bad feeling about this particular meeting, since receiving the invitation a few days ago. Even after so many, many meetings, this one seemed different somehow, though why she couldn't say. After all, logically she had nothing to worry about. They were doing better than ever, yet as the days drew closer the illogical feeling of absolute dread was almost tangible where it hung over the two of them like a ghost.

But why? Why was the question. What, with the publishing of the quarterly suggestopedic journal running for three years now in three separate languages plus the overall popularity and the success of the institute had gained Georgi a group of supporters along with his ever loyal patients who loved him dearly. They should feel almost invincible and this point, yet were she to ask him she was almost certain he would tell her that he was actually nervous about this.

Just a few months ago, the Sofia international expert meeting of UNESCO had taken place. The purpose had been for the experts to explore the place the methodology in the education system, for all age groups. So many specialists had come...

All had been given the opportunity to observe the study process and even test the children. The conclusion was unanimous. Having won them over by a landslide, the committee was very impressed. As a result, a decision was made for the suggestopedic system to be applied in all the schools in Bulgaria, starting with Mihailovgrad. A true landmark in their work, that should have been a triumph and indeed was; but that triumph had been spoiled by a new shadow that came to loom over them in recent days, a circle of psychiatrists, educators, philosophers, and university lecturers who were against the work.

Perhaps it was envy, or fear that something new had entered their territory. In the changing times, traditional methods often might be over looked for something new or better. Whatever the case, the success had been a catalyst for a whole new world of stress. Negative articles had begun to circulate in the daily newspapers, like Vecherni Novini. Authors like Popvasilev, Ganchev and others well known voices in the country had voiced their speculation if not outright disbelief in their methodology.

Responses had been made, of course. Questions answered to the best of their ability, all while keeping up a friendly tone, despite the insults. Unlike those who pointed fingers and whispered open slurs in their articles, Dr. Lozanov had made certain not to answer in kind. Instead, he composed his response with the dignity and gravitas that was just simply the man he was. Never mind that it was misinterpreted, disputed and outright ignored by his naysayers. No matter how often they hurt him, he was always willing to turn the other cheek. It was something she had admired in him from the very beginning, and still did even today.

"Do you think we should cancel?" She asked after a while of saying nothing at all. He shook his head negatively, almost instantly.

"What kind of man would I be to embrace the good and run from the bad," he chuckled low in his throat then shook his head once more. "No." He sighed. "We will go. For good, or ill. It's the right thing to do." And it was. She knew it as well as he did. Now, if only that feeling would prove to be nothing but nerves and all would go well. If only, though they both doubted it. Regardless, the days drew closer bit by bit, she knew they would take it head on, for good, or bad as it would be. She only hoped it was the former.

CHAPTER 14

Much like that first convention all those years ago, the days leading up to the big event were tense and unsettled, with Dr. Georgi and Dr. Evelina doing their level best not to argue with each other in the midst of all the stress and emotion. However, it was hard and they just wanted it all to be over. Finally, it was here. The day was upon them with tension never higher and a cold sweat shared between them. It almost seemed like every waking moment they had shared together was leading up to this singular thing, though they both knew that to be an over exaggeration of emotion. Come what may, they would endure and eventually triumph, they both agreed, but the waiting was still very hard for both of them.

"We will call to order the meeting, now that everyone is present." The tall man announced to the room at large. Everyone nodded. Some seemed almost as anxious as he was, while others were cool and collected as he tried to present himself. For them however, it wasn't an act and he began to wonder if this was how a rabbit felt when being stalked by some sort of predatory animal. It was a chilling experience, to say the least.

"Dr. Lozanov, you have the floor." The announcer dictated, gesturing toward the man as he stood. A cursory round of applause filled the chamber but as the doctor took his place, he was struck by the funniest feeling that it wasn't him they were cheering for. All eyes were on him, surrounding the spotlight with a gaze that ranged anywhere from speculative to skeptical and anywhere in between.

Taking in a breath, he sighed to see at least a few familiar faces, the 10th year students who had participated in the language study. Their parents and teachers as well as a few notable voices of the day attended. Lecturers, students, and professors of all fields had turned out for the conference, as usual. Unlike the many other times however, it was plain to all in attendance that something amiss. Perhaps the air was too tight in the room, making everyone feel slight sense of claustrophobia. Maybe it was only the doctor, projecting his white-hot nerves onto the house at large. Who could be certain?

The full house was all eyes as Dr. Lozanov was called to speak. The prepared notes were only guidelines for talking points and the like. By now, he was more than comfortable with speech making and speaking to crowds, despite the unusual stress. Calm, at least in voice, his comfortable, confident speech addressed the room in a friendly, almost familiar manner. After all, most all of them had been here at least one before. As serene as he presented himself they would never know the way his legs shook slightly or how his heart raced.

"Now to begin." He smiled numbly. But where? At the source of the problem, one would assume but it was so much more complicated than that. So much so that he found himself talking for a long time. Longer than he wanted to by far, yet as topics were addressed, and questions put to rest, he knew from the sour expressions in the crowed that it was not near long enough. The words "thank you," were barely spoken at the conclusion of the address before the chaos erupted. People shouted at him from all sides in a tidal wave of questions, angry accusations and vehement denial from all around rushed at him all at once. Teachers quickly hushed students who stood, seemingly to defend the doctor against the verbal assault.

A man shouted a question from the front row. "Well, as for that," the doctor began just as another cut him off, words running right over him. "As I stated before," he tried, only to be shouted at from across the room again, this time by a woman. "If you would let me explain," He tried desperately. Not a friendly face seemed to look back at him from the crowd as he swallowed his nerves and tried again.

The effort was to no avail. Groundless questions were slung at him over and over, one right after another before he had time to answer the first. People talked over him, under him and above him until he was unheard by even himself, voice vanishing in the cacophony of chaos.

He could see his Evelina frowning from her corner and longed to rush to her and take her hand, though he knew he could not. Finally, Professor Ganev stood and put a stop to the chaos, with his loud booming voice, calling the room to order with a few short words.

"Now," he said evenly, once all were calmed and seated once more. "I think now it would be best to hear from the 10th grade students, who have been taught suggestopedically throughout the year in all subjects."

A gesture was made toward a group of excited-looking youngsters who had been mostly unnoticed until just then. Taking the floor, each child gave their opinion of the learning process with a level of enthusiasm that should have warmed even the coldest of skeptics. Zealous in their speech they gladly enlightened the room at large. Each was adamant that they were happy studying with the system, that all the acquisition was easy. Some even admonished those that had spoken against the doctor, which was quite the bold move for such youngsters. It made Dr. Lozanov smile too see it and here the sincerity in their strong young voices, though he hoped it would not reflect poorly on the children.

Without tension or homework, and all the material learned only during the study period, the children proudly showed their grade books that proved them to be at the top of their grades. Looking out onto the crowd now, it was easy to see some contemplate a change of mind while others carved their frowns from blocks of granite.

That, coupled with the absolute indignation that the other professors could behave in a similar way was near enough to have Evelina in tears as she watched silently from her little corner. Georgi on the other hand stood proudly and strong ... center stage as the children took their seats. From there the discussion came to a rapid close, thanks to Professor Ganev. Sullen faces filed out one at a time, obviously disgruntled while others clapped the good doctor on the shoulder for a job well done.

Perhaps it had not been the doom the both expected to be and indeed, it seemed to have turned out all right but Georgi was glad it was over. So was Evelina, he noticed as she finally made her was to him to stand by his side while the others convened around them with the Dr. Lozanov the center of attention. New faces showed themselves amongst the hustle and bustle, each timidly coming to speak to the man they had doubted so severely not but an hour or so before.

One man even went so far as to shaking his hand and offer his apologies for misjudged assumptions. Apparently encouraged by the gentle reception the man received, others chimed in as well with their own ostensibly heartfelt apologies. Dr. Lozanov beamed at them all. It was a small battle, but a battle nonetheless that they had won. Triumph and perseverance had won the day and would continue to lead them over the next week or two.

Chapter 15

Where the top of one hill was reached, in glorious triumph, another obstacle cast a shadow on the newly won victory. It was much like in the early days of the institution where whispers followed him wherever he went, not only on the street, but also in the workplace. The working ambiance was worsening, reflecting on the team at the institute. To aggravate it all, some of his colleagues had begun to develop negative attitude toward Georgi and Evelina working so closely together. Some were even jealous and tried to discourage his trust in her. He would of course not explain the fact that she was not only necessary to the methodology, but to he himself as a man. Not that he had to explain himself.

Why, just the other day he had heard a few gossiping about the two of them where the gossip mongers thought Georgi could not overhear.

Even Lyudmila Zhivkova, the daughter of the President, had made a comment on the relationship. "We know that you and comrade Gateva are together but we think that you are doing very good things. Rumors have reached even us, but do not worry!"

At least there were some blessings to be had.

In this day and time, with the current political ideology frowning upon them more so than the majority of their coworkers, the voice of a higher approval was good news. Good news indeed, though they both knew it didn't make a difference. They were both beyond the age of seeking approval of such things from their peers. If wandering minds chose to pass judgment over their personal lives, even though it never once touched upon their professional business, well, so be it. There were much worse things in the world to worry about than prying busy bodies.

What with one thing after another hindering and harrying them at every turn, a few gossips certainly weren't going to hurt them. As always, they would stand strong. That did not mean, however, that those against them, including some higher-ups did not try to part them as often as possible. Georgi could not even travel abroad for conferences with Evalina, without someone suggesting he take someone *else* to accompany him, which was ridiculous. Even had they been nothing but partners, she was essential to both him and the work. Other than Georgi she knew the methodology better than anyone else did after having developed much of the key workings herself and was simply not a person he could afford to leave at home just to appease someone else.

To the rest of the world, up until she attained her degree, she might have been no one to them but to him, she had always been his everything. The others simply didn't like that she was a no one, from a small city in the North part of Bulgaria with no gilded family name or great wealth to put her up to their standards. Instead she had to actually *work* to get where she was today, forever by his side and it galled some to the bone that they simply could not insinuate themselves into the highly coveted space that was now he's. He'd even been advised by some to "look around" and perhaps survey other options.

As if, there were any other options. Even with his staff, being composed daughters, sisters and cousins from the old aristocracy, there was no one who came close, no matter how much they might wish it. Unfortunately, however this also meant that it was quite easy for some to have hurt feelings over it all. However, what did he care? He had the only thing he needed.

For her talent and devotion to him, her beautiful soul, and a giving nature, he knew in his heart where this relationship was going and where his heart would lead him. Of course, he would follow. She was his light. She was his window into the world.

A window that was sorely needed just then, as sad eyes looked out into a rain swamped Sofia.

He sighed.

"I have already told you, you cannot resign." She frowned at him over her book. The tea was cold. She had poured it for him an hour ago and he'd done nothing but pace around the desk, nursing the worry that had them both up and about so late. Again.

"And I have heard you," Georgi's frown mirrored her own as he sank into a high backed chair. "But I still do not see why not." There was that look again. She hated to see it on his face, that sad eyed sorrow. It seemed that was all she ever saw from him anymore.

"Is it so unbearable?" Her voice was soft as she put down her papers to look at him with sad eyes. For a little while, he didn't say anything. The little wall clock counted almost a quarter hour before he finally spoke, his voice strained.

"Would you think less of me," He frowned at her with heartbreaking eyes of green. "If I said yes?" The eyes that met hers now were something she had never seen before. Something of one ready to give up. Her heart sank to the floor.

"I would not think less of you," the musician answered softly, shaking her delicate little head. "But what will *you* think of you? That is the question." A question she had asked him the last time this same, sad issue had come up.

Repeatedly, he had told her he was just going to resign and give it all up. The little victories didn't seem to matter. The conferences, the interest and positive response as a whole over the past few years…

none of it seemed to matter to him when he got into one of these strange moods. She knew just as he was looking at her that he did not mean it. He couldn't give up the work anymore than he could stop breathing. It was that much a part of who and what he was. Just as a sad weight crushed his strong shoulders into the chair, so would it lift again to let him stand tall and proud once more. If, he didn't up and do something rash in the meantime, such as resign his post, as he had been threatening to do for days now.

"What do they think of me, is the question, I think." His voice was solemn. Long his fingers dandled a loose fiber, caught on the fabric of the chair. She watched it with fascination for a moment, waiting for him to finish the thought. "It should not matter, I know I know." The doctor sighed. "But it does. I am like this thread here, you see?"

She watched as he held it up to the light. "They pull and pull. I stand," he paused, demonstrating the strength of the material with one hand while the other gestured to illustrate his point. "But over time, the thread weakens. Starts to strain…" Again, he pulled, thinning out the body of the fabric until it snapped with a little *popping* sound.

Once a teacher; always a teacher. Now that his point was made, she watched his posture flatten once more into a deflated slump. "And then what? Then I will be broken, good for nothing. What then?" With a shake of his snowy head, he slouched even further into the cushioned chair, looking older and more tired than she thought she had ever seen her beloved Georgi.

"So…" She sighed herself now, reaching out a hand to take his. Their fingers linked a familiar way of one soul to another, the kind of touch that went beyond the physical to something else. Repeatedly she wished she could reach that something else and sooth it or strengthen it, giving her dearest the strength he seemed to lack just then. It was to no avail. Instead, they just sat in the sad, companionable silence, contemplating it all. "Is this it then?" She whispered, finally speaking when she could stand the silence no more. "Do we just give up?" Surely not. Not after all this time, all these years.

"What else is there to do?" The doctor took a sharp, pained breath.

"Well…you could always keep going?" She suggested. In truth, there was nothing else that would happen. He would, eventually prevail; rising up from the gloom like a shining hero to gallantly beat back the opposition. Eventually. Tonight though, tonight was a night for grey melancholy, something she knew he needed once in a while, when it all became too much. As much as she hated it. As much as it hurt her to her very soul to watch him, like this…She would abide and allow him the time for grief and doubt. Everyone needed it, after all. Even the great genius and heroes of the world.

"After all, you have already tried to resign three times now. What makes you think a fourth will do you any better?" She smiled now, squeezing his hand where it held her own. "Besides. You know they need you." He should anyway, but the skeptical glance he gave her said otherwise. "Humph." She scoffed at him, grinning now. "You know it is true. Why else would they not have let you leave?"

"I don't know," he grumbled, looking very much like a little child being scolded, even as he cracked a grin his way. "Perhaps to keep you in line so you do not cause trouble?" The doctor jibed, laughing at her mock indignation. She laughed too; glad to see him finally coming out of his blue mood. She hated these nights like this, but the moment he would finally smile at her was worth every one of them.

That smile faded suddenly, melting into nothing as his face paled to pure white. "Georgi?" Her voice was urgent as she called his name. "What is wrong?"

"Pain…oh the pain…" he gasped, hands clutching at his chest as he tried to breath. "Pain in my chest…" For a split second, she felt the world drop and fall out from under her as she realized what must have been happening. "Quickly…" he motioned toward the phone, even as she reached to dial the number.

The ambulance was there in a matter of moments. Red lights cut through the quiet of the night as people gathered around to find out what had happened. Staff members, co-workers, and colleagues alike watched in mute horror as their director was taken out on a stretcher, white-faced Evelina in their wake.

****

After several hours of hand wringing anxiety, they finally called her. Almost no one had spoken a word to her the whole time and of course, she was not allowed to see him, so she nearly fainted when they called her. Was he alright? After all this, where they going to tell her that he was…no, no. She would not, could not think about it. Swallowing her heart, she approached the white coated doctor with his little clipboard, fear plain on her face. "Yes?"

A heart attack. According to the young man, it was not uncommon for a man of his age, especially under as much stress as he had been. His age? He was only 53!

After a long while of explanations she did not need and a lot of reassurance, they let her in. "Only for a moment," a stern looking nurse cautioned, frowning as if she made it her life's mission to disturb the peace of the patients. He was sleeping. It didn't occur to her until just then just how tired he must have been. The way his face looked now, free of any frown or furrowed wrinkle of disquiet was a shock. It had been so long since she had seen anything but the stress and strain on his face, she scarcely recognized him.

"Oh, my poor love," she whispered, leaning down to brush a kiss across his temple. Would it be wrong to cry now, she wondered? It seemed terribly unfair. After all, he was the one under so much strain and he did not cry. Even now…A heart attack! Perhaps it really was so unbearable and yet he stayed strong. Even in his sleep, she could see his strength. How could she not? Perhaps he could lend her a bit of that strength as she held his hand. Then she would not cry… Not much anyway.

With another kiss to say goodbye, she turned on her heel just in time to see the sour faced woman had returned. It was time to go. Someone suggested she might try to go home and get some sleep. She thanked them kindly for the advice, knowing that was all she could do. If she were to see any sleep at all in the next few days, it would be a miracle. She didn't have time for any of that. No, no, her time would be put toward the work in the daytime and to visiting her beloved whenever she wasn't working. Maybe then, she might have some done for him for when it would be time for him to go home.

Yes, of course. It was a perfect idea. That way she could keep her mind busy and not give in to the urge to weep that loomed over her shoulder at the sudden fear that he might not be coming home. Which, of course, he was. He had to. It was not just the people at the institute who needed him, or the students. Not even his fellow teachers crossed her mind, just then. Perhaps it was a selfish thing to realize that most of all *she* needed him.

Chapter 16

After watching him recover from the heart attack, Evelina watched her precious doctor for months after the incident. Unsurprisingly however he recovered almost instantly, strong and healthy which he constantly attributed to her care, though she knew it was his strength that carried him, not her own.

After a long enough time, once the doctors and Evelina both were satisfied with his progress it was decided that they probably be getting back to their work and plans were made to travel. There were quite a few conferences and lectures that had been missing them over the month or two, so it would be good to get back into the swing of things, especially with all the rumors flying about the good doctor's sudden absence.

Packed, passports in and smiling, the pair made their way to the airport with jolly, jubilant smiles.

Those smiles vanished however in the face of a tall, sallow skinned man as he tucked their passports away into his pocket it with a smile.

Surely, there was a mistake. There must be a misunderstanding, she told herself, willing her face to remain blank. To the front of them stood the sour looking man with a comb-over and a pinched smile, none too gently ordering them to return home. Behind them, a small crowd of onlookers, halted in place to watch the goings on. It had been bad enough to have stepped into the building and see several people stop and point but of course, something was unavoidable. After all, who didn't see the famous Dr. Georgi Lozanov and not know who he was, for some reason or another. Unfortunately, for their sake, that reputation wasn't always a good thing. Whispers followed them both in and out of the airport.

At first, all had seemed fine. Everything was as it should be, as they laughed and talked amongst themselves while they waited in line. Nothing was out of the ordinary, up until they were asked for their passports. This wasn't the first time they had traveled out of the country together. Everything seemed like standard procedure until they were asked to wait.

Strange, yes they both agreed but nothing too out of the ordinary. Then security showed up with the snarling, pale-skinned man and his sour look. Their passports were taken and after several rude questions they weren't even allowed to answer, they were released. Go home, they were told. Do not try to travel again and no, they could not have their papers back. Instead, they were to march right back out, in front of all those watchful eyes and ears.

"They cannot do this!" Georgi stormed, slapping his leg in fury. Evelina winced, wondering what this stress must be doing to him. Would it possibly end him back up in the hospital? She paled at the thought. "This is completely outrageous!" He continued, unaware of her worry.

That it was, she agreed to the first. No point in refuting the second. "Try to calm down please," she urged, laying her hand over his where it held the wheel of the car in an iron grip.

They both knew perfectly well *the party* most certainly could do whatever they pleased and no one could do anything about it. It shouldn't have been a surprise, she pointed out to him once he was calm. The look he shot her was one of those that said while he agreed, he didn't like it. Not at all. Years of treading on the thin ice of the party's toes, pushing the boundaries of what their rigid system would allow. No, indeed it shouldn't have been a surprise. So why were they both so shocked now?

Well, timing could have something to do with it. Why now? After so much progress, practically unhindered why had they decided to step in now? Not that they *knew* that was the reason they had been denied passage, at least, not because someone had told them. They hadn't been told anything at all and doubted that would change. No point in it though, really. Everyone knew. Not only did they fully well know that it was because of their work, but also so did everyone else in that airport.

It was infuriating, the way their close-minded government was determined to crush everything they worked so hard for. As though all of that was not enough, now this. "This changes nothing," the white haired doctor remarked, once he was calm. "We will continue our work, regardless."

In as much as they could. Over the next few months however, it would be harder and harder to keep that determined outlook as every attempt to make contact with the scientific world was thwarted. Not only could they not travel or communicate with foreigners, even their lectures had been stopped. No papers could be written, none of the conferences that had invitations piling in day by day could be attended. Even the film director from Hamburg, come to make a film about the work was denied.

The reasoning? Dr. Lozanov was ill. Never mind he was in the best of health, save a noted (and understandable) increase in stress. To the rest of the world, he was bedridden and unable to be seen by anyone. This was the answer given to the number of inquiries as to his whereabouts, how to get in touch with him and as to when the rest of the world would be seeing more about the work. The conference in Moscow as well, much to everyone's dismay.

And of course, while no work could be done or even completed, the vicious newspaper attacks were allowed to continue, blackening the reputation of both the man and his work without even the chance for defense. Experiments began to fail as a plague of lies rumors began to spread. People began to avoid the institute and its doings, rather than seek it out.

Despite all of this, even with the new ridicule they had to endure and the absolute lack of support from anyone who still had the ability to speak against it and defend them, they continued to work.

"I have a bad feeling about all of this," Evelina whispered, one day just as they were both coming into work.

"What sort of feeling?" Georgi frowned, had frozen where his keys had lifted to let them in. Earliest to arrive and latest to leave, as always they were the only two around for what seemed like miles. The pristine sterility of sparkling hallways and waxed floors gleamed uncomfortably clean in her peripheral vision as she stepped closer.

"The kind that says things are only about to get worse," she sighed.

For a long moment, they frowned, not so much at each other, but together in the pregnant pause that seemed to be the quiet before the storm. He too could feel the looming disquiet; ever near as it had been since they had been turned away from the airport. Today, however it seemed closer than ever.

"So." He looked at her, lifting a finger to push up his glasses where they liked to creep down the bridge of this nose. "What can I do? Run from it?" He shook his head. "I will not be a coward."

"Oh course not," was her immediate answer. "But could you not be more cautious?"

Georgi laughed, almost bitterly. "Who leans on the side of caution when they know they have nothing to lose?" Well, that indeed was a question. After all, if something horrible did lie beyond the door waiting for them, then it was already too late. "Why not just push through, and know it will all be alright?"

There was that smile again. That confidence. She nodded and caught his hand with hers, giving in a squeeze before they both straightened their shoulders and pushed through the door. No one was there, of course and they went about the morning as always. That ominous feeling never left, not even for a moment, but it wasn't until much later in the day that they were to see it come to fruit.

It was 10 minutes before the lunch break, when she saw them. Alexander Fol, the minister of education was marching toward Dr. Lozanov, along with Radka Makedonska from the central committee of the communist party. Just the sight of them made her heart sink with the realization she had been right. Something was about to happen. Excusing herself from her discussion, she began making her way to the scene in hopes of beating the dreadful duo to her beloved doctor.

Alas, she was too late. The pair had halted and politely tapped the man on the shoulder, as if asking for the time. The expression that crossed his face was one of pleasant surprise, much better than the dread that leaked through her transparent visage. *Thump, thump, thump...* her heart raced in time with her footsteps as she made the last few steps, just in time to hear them at the top of their lungs.

"By order of decision from the central committee of the communist party, Dr. Georgi Lozanov, we hereby dismiss you as director from the Institute of Suggestology."

The room was silent. Every face looked to Dr. Lozanov with heartbroken shock. You would have thought it had been all of them to have been removed from several years' worth of back breaking work, in front of a room full of colleagues. It did not matter how close you had been standing, or how far. Everyone had heard it.

With that news delivered, the two turned to toward Dr. Rumiana Noncheva who was apparently herself no where near qualified to become director. Little less than a year before, she had been suspected of fraud in the form of plagiary of the suggestopedic works. The scientific council had made the decision to take away her title as a PhD holder and even dismiss her from the institute. Instead, she was to become the director.

While Evelina doubted things could get more outrageous at this point, she was begging to wonder at the sanity of her country's government and the people in charge of it, but never mind those people. More important than any of them was her beloved Georgi, who now stood with the shocked look of someone who had been smacked across the face with a week old fish?

"Are you alright?" She asked him quietly as the rest of the room milled about dumbly, as though nothing had happened.

"I do not know," he said honestly, shaking his head. "I do not know."

Chapter 17

ᥫ᭡

The long hallway was quiet, save for the sound of footsteps walking along side each other, one soft and quiet, the other strong and confident. It had been a long day for the two of them, longer than either one of them could have hoped, but after what they had endured over the last several months, nothing came as a surprise to them any longer. Since Dr. Lozanov's termination from his own institute, something that still galled them both even after a month after the fact, things had not been the same.

Years of working together, 7 days a week and 12 to 13 hours a day had cultivated a specific and very careful routine between the two of them that had been as much a part of their partnership as the work itself. Now, instead of rising to meet the early morning, even before dawn broke it's gaze across the early morning sky and working until long after everyone else had gone home, now there was nothing.

Or so it had seemed at first. Without that comfortable schedule shared between them life seemed almost empty and yet, with each day as they searched for somewhere else to begin again, they learned to live a little bit at a time. It was a slow, almost daunting process and at times seemed impossible but they both knew, given enough time they would get used to it. The university at least, had taken some responsibility and placed them in an upper, more worn part of the building, giving the good doctor some sort of superficial title and position, almost as if apologizing for their wrong doing.

In reality, they both knew that it would be a waste on the college's part to simply fire them, but they also didn't want him having any position of importance any time soon. Waste not, want not, as the saying went and Dr. Lozanov knew it was true and knew there was nothing they could do about it. There was nowhere else they could go, they knew, after trying to find a replacement work space for a solid month.

In the meantime between the incident and the new "position" , the search for a new headquarters and work space was constant, filling the gap of loss with phone calls, long explanations and ultimately disappointment as they were refused time and time again. No one would take them. Why, they weren't sure but they both suspected it had something to do with the party and their tight hold over the educational system. It was a horribly, horribly depressing prospect, one that had him wanting to throw up his hands at any given turn.

Worse yet was to see that as they struggled and fought to stay afloat, their precious institute went on without them, seemingly unmissed or noticed. It was a deep shock to the pride and even deeper to the heart to realize that even after all those years of work, some people were still only in the business for the paycheck, and not the love of the work itself.

Never the less, despite disappointment after disappointment they persevered as always, searching for what seemed forever. Finally, when it seemed like all hope was lost they struck upon bit of good luck, just as they were settling in to the new place.

"And she will not let you take anything with you?" Evelina asked for the third time, already knowing the answer yet still unable to believe the audacity of it. The question echoed through the hallway of the Sofia University with incredulous skepticism and anger. The doctor shook his head and sighed, long and hard.

"Nothing! Not even the notes from the Clairvoyant experiments, or the film from Vanga." Now they both sighed, practically in unison as unshed anger and frustration clenched the doctor's gentle fists.

"So, what are we going to do now?" Evelina's face was skeptical in the dim light of the poorly lit corridor.

It was not looking good for them, today, nor had it been, any other day since they had been forced to leave. Not if they were going to have to start all over again, from scratch. Dr. Lozanov knew the prospect was dismal, just as he knew it was not going to be easy. Then again, come to think of it, when had it ever been easy? When had it ever been anything than the back breaking work that it was, even when things where in the peak of prosperity and fruitfulness? When had it ever been anything but his communist government, clenching their iron fist over anything that was new, inventive and not their own idea? Never. Never had it been and never would it be, so long as he was oppressed by his tyrannical government and their collective hate for anything that might actually do the country, if not the world some real good.

It made him angry to think of all the people he could be helping, if others did not stand in their way and all the good that could be done, if they only had that one, little chance. Was it to be like this always? Always working in secret, or against the odds that were not only unfair, but unnatural in that they were obstacles forced by his fellow man, and not the usually occurrences that might hinder a person, such as age or ill health. Had it been the natural causes that kept him from his lifelong love, then perhaps he could have accepted it a bit more gently, but this? This was outrageous. To be stopped, stomped and hindered at every turn, no matter what he was doing, no matter what the reason was truly painful to him! Truly. He wanted nothing more than to do good across the world. To love and share that love with all so that they too would understand that love, was the key too all.

"We do the best we can," he smiled. Tired eyes kicked up at the corners for just a moment as he looked at her then flickered and faded again. None of this had been easy for them, over the last month or so. They had fought once or twice. He had snapped at her over something silly and she had snapped back. As soon as it had happened though, the effect was almost instant, and they had spent at least an hour afterwards apologizing to one another. Then they talked. Talked about life and love and love for each other. Harkening back to younger days. "Do you remember when I had wanted to get married to you," he had smiled boyishly as she looked at him.

She laughed. "Yes, and they you were terribly hurt when I turned you down." Rose cheeks dimpled charmingly as she reached for his hand. "But then I explained why and you were not hurt any longer."

"Or maybe I was," He winked. "And just didn't tell you."

She gasped and frowned. "We're you really?" Her eyes saddened.

"Ah, maybe for a small time," the doctor had admitted, then smiled. "But how could I stay hurt long. So long as I have you, what name should I call it, for you to be mine?" He laughed, linking her fingers with him. "Even if I still think it was silly."

"It wasn't silly," she smiled gently. "If there were no children, then I still see no reason for marriage." She said in a matter of fact manner, still maintaining the opinion she had when he had asked her years ago.

He still didn't agree to it, but knew there was no arguing with her, once her mind had been made up and in all honestly, so long as they were together and not fighting, what did he care? If they were not married in name, then surely in heart, just as they had been since the very beginning. Whether fighting, calm, sick, well, or indifferent, she was his and he was hers. Yes, certainly, even trying as hard as they had, tempers had been short now and again. It couldn't be helped, in moments like this but all in all, they had done well. If nothing else, by sheer force of will alone, they had only fought once since the dismissal from the institute and over something petty. Since then, things had been as they always had been, if perhaps a little more strained, of course.

"The best we can seems like a lot more than it used to," Evelina sighed almost longingly, thinking of the days before. It had never been 'easy', but as the hallway came to a sudden stop with a road block of dingy glass doors she could remember a time it certainly was *easier*. The difference was stark, reflected in both their tired faces.

Years' worth of work, wear and tear could be seen, etched plainly into eyes that always tried to look tireless when in truth they were exhausted.

"Do you regret it?" He asked quietly, turning to meet her eyes. It wasn't a question, as far as she could see, shaking her head.

"Do you?" She smiled, finding her answer returned duly. "Well then, there is your answer."

"Well then." The doctor sighed softly, relieved by her answer more than he could say and took out his key. The door opened to with the kind of anticlimactic screech that seemed far too fitting for such a dim prospect. "Home sweet home," He chuckled half-heartedly. "Shall we begin?"

The answer poised on both their frowning mouths was of course 'no'. No, they did not want to begin all over again. No, they did not want to work long days with long hours, very little sleep and even less respect for their efforts. No, they did not want to do this all over again.

But that was not an answer or even an option so no one spoke. Instead, they simply nodded to one another and began the long haul back toward normalcy.

Two rooms to house 11 people, no desks, no shelves, not even chairs were to be had in the hobnail little circus that became the new and as of yet, unnamed Scientific research laboratory.

To anyone who could have just wandered in, they would have seen the strangest congress of several grown individuals sitting on stacks of text books as courses were lectured. But had you stepped in, you would have seen those aforementioned patrons of the most respectful variety.

Backs were straight. Eyes and ears were front and center with the respect for the teacher that was neither expected, nor demanded. Simply given as the gift it was from one human to the next. Never mind their station was a taped together box on chairs of molding literature.

This was a world class lesson with the class of the world as head of the proceedings.

Grudgingly those involved evolved to the stress and began to work well with the environment. Quite a leap indeed, but well worth it. Whether the two or three who were on fixed salary or the majority who were self- supported, the results of the work negated most everything, including pay or the lack thereof. This was well beyond money. Those involved were there for a reason.

If nothing else, perhaps the chance to see it all work out and reach that potential they all struggled toward.

They wouldn't have to wait long.

A month or three, give or take and things began to settle in to what seemed to be the new norm. Then, one humid day, just at the beginning of the week, Prof. Mincho Semov, the rector of the University of Sofia decided to pay the group a visit.

While unprepared and not likely to be any less so any time soon, Dr. Lozanov managed to scrap together a reasonable approximation of a tour.

All was smiles and laughs, until the professor actually spoke. "This is ridiculous," the man stormed, after just the slightest glance at the conditions the team was forced to work under.

"It's better than nothing." The doctor shrugged with a humble sort of smile. "We do what we can, with what we have."

"Well," the professor harrumphed himself up to his full height to loom ominously over the room at large. "Dr. Lozanov, I would appreciate it if you would step out into the hall with me, for just a moment." The old man rumbled, looking very much like an old tired walrus that was out of sorts. Dr. Lozanov coughed politely in effort hid his smile and shake that sudden imagery out of his mind, before nodding his acquiescence. The entire room looking around nervously at one another as the two men shuffled out of the tiny space.

The long hallway was quiet, as ever, this time without the echoing steps. Pipes groaned somewhere off in the distance as the two men eyed each other for a moment.

The older man coughed. "Your termination was absolutely preposterous." He said, shaking his head and pacing just a little, as though deep in thought. "I cannot believe the way things are handled, in this day and age." He continued.

"Your dismissal was foolishness of the most extreme," the man explained, herding the entire team up and out of their make shift stations. The troop was lead to a different building all together, a newer brick building just near the Pliska hotel.

The entire story of the building that was empty as far as the eye could see and with more windows than the last it made the whole place a little brighter. Cleaner too, Dr. Lozanov was happy to note, taking in the lack of cobwebs and dangling spiders with a smile.

"You will work here." It wasn't a question and they were in no position to argue. With a whole story of the building to themselves, they could begin the *real* work.

Everyone thanked the professor profoundly before finding and organizing their *station*. In just a short few weeks, between the new space they had gained and about a months' worth of back breaking work, enough money was gained for the barest of essentials.

Furniture or at least a better mock up of such gave them better ability to organize and finally, the independent Center of Suggestology and Development of Personality at the University of Sofia was born.

Chapter 18

§🔊

1989

Elation! Elation was the feeling that rushed over him, warm and heady as he held his passport in one hand, and a plane ticket in the other. Beside him, his partner and love stood smiling wide and bright with hands full of much the same.

It had happened. The moment so many had hoped for and dreamed for had finally come. The communist regime was removed from power. For them and the rest of the world, the removal of the Iron Curtain meant the isolation was over, for everyone.

For Georgi and Evelina it meant house arrest had been lifted and their rights returned to them fully. Not only could they publish and lecture once more, but now they could come and go as they pleased. The world was open to them again, finally.

The first stop on the list was Moscow, then Tokyo to demonstrate 10 years' worth of hard work and the new Dessuggestive methodology. What a feeling! There was no way to describe it. Not even elation was a proper word and as they marched through the line, one at a time he knew he'd never be able to articulate the moment to another living soul.

If you did not know what it meant to be finally free again after years of separation from the rest of the world, then it was not something you could be told. If you did not live through it, you did not and could not ever know what it meant. If you did not live through it, you were lucky. It was a thing you had to know for yourself, and he hoped as long as he lived he would never know it again.

Yes, the stories they would tell would be sad and sometimes horrific. The memories, still sharp would always be the talking point, in times of quiet. But no matter who told you what, what you heard, what you did or didn't think...no matter what, you could never actually know and so long as he lived, be it one more day or one hundred more years, he hoped that he never knew it again.

"Aren't you excited?" Evelina beamed as they boarded the airplane. Excitement, yes! Of course he was excited, if the warmth in his chest and brightness of his eyes were any sign. "A bit, yes" he nodded enthusiastically. But, he was also worried. Knowing the circles he and his work ran in and how inactivity on his part could turn in to disinterest for the rest of the world.

There was some fear to be had. Fear of how their forced suspension might have damned their working relationships with the other countries. Or how much cleanup they would end up doing? How much disinterest had their absence generated. Without being around to constantly stir the waters, he was afraid the tide had taken off without them, leaving them and their work to dry out on the shore of the inactive, washed up and failed. It was a terrible thing to consider.

Rumors had been flying around, for over a year now, about something that sounded very similar to his work, yet wildly different. The process had been sped up or amplified in the name of convenience. Supposedly faster or better, these distorted methods were being developed a dime a dozen and taught to hapless people without any understanding of what they were doing. Bad enough that they were stealing and abusing his painstakingly created process. What of the people that could be damaged by this?

It made him ill to think of the harm it could be doing to the so called 'students' and while imitation was the best form of flattery, there was quite a bit more than ego at stake here. If things were not handled properly, there was no telling the destruction that could be done or if it was even fixable. While amazing, extraordinary, and to his belief, almost limitless, the human mind was tender thing and he knew if some person or persons were damaged due to this, he would never be able to forgive himself for not being there to see that it was handled properly.

"I am a bit excited," he admitted, smiling as they took their seats. As the plane began to take off and his heart thudded with adrenaline he wondered what was in store for them next. Linking hands with one another, they both took a deep breath. It was more than the sudden change of gravity that had them both tightening in their seats. This was it. This trip could make or break their reintroduction into the world and they knew it must be handled carefully. It wasn't every day a person vanished for 10 years, and then suddenly showed back up again. Would they have to do a lot of catch up to find their old standing? Or would they be well received at the conference?

These were questions that weighed heavily on both their minds through the long flight. To pass the time, they made plans for the presentation and what topics to cover while they were at it. The usual check list was looked over and double checked, just to be sure. Explanations for the absence were discussed as well.

It was a touchy subject all in all and while they knew they could now tell the world the truth, they weren't sure they wanted to. Old habits were difficult to change.

The hours passed easily, floating by on a discussion of lecture topics and shared laughter. With so much to do and so little time to do it in, the flight was over and the plane was touching down before they knew it. Looking out the window, Georgi found his heart oddly heavy, considering the circumstances. After so long, it was almost overwhelming to jump back into the scientific circus once more. His head swam with delighted aggravation even now, already anticipating the late nights and early mornings that they would soon be getting used to again.

Not, mind you that they had slipped that far from the routine, but it was quite a bit different to wake up with the dawn in your own bed as opposed to all over the world. Business traveling was stressful, worrisome and unduly exhausting, be it overnight to a conference or to another country entirely for a week long affair. Who knew what they would be doing or even when and if they averaged a solid four hours sleep the whole time, they would be lucky. They both knew this and knew it well. Worst of all was that after all this time, it sounded positively lovely.

Once they arrived in snowy Moscow however, he found he had other things on his mind. Namely the sight of his beautiful Evelina dappled in the lightly falling snow and smiling at him. Cheeks pinked where the harsh winter wind had colored any exposed flesh, she was as bright as the city lights that greeted them from a far.

He smiled, even as cold as it was he felt a sudden warmth and lightness where cold leaden weight had sat before. It was quite a wonderful shock to realize that despite everything, she had stayed with him through all of this.

The ridicule. The rumors spread by friend and foe alike. The heart attack and the house arrest and yet, regardless, she was still standing here, with him.

"Do you remember the letter I sent you, from Japan?" He asked softly, almost shyly as they drove from the airport to the hotel. It felt strange to talk about such things, now, when they had so much else to worry about and yet, he couldn't think of a better time.

"Yes," she said simply. Even with her head turned toward the window and watching the world go by, he could hear the smile in her voice.

"You remember when I wrote to you that you were my window to the world?" Taking her hand in his, the doctor sighed warmly. "You still are, you know. Without you, through all this…I would be sightless. Blind. But you…" he lifted her hand just enough to brush the gentlest of kisses across her palm, before giving it a light squeeze. "You let the light into my life."

The last was spoken as a whisper. He let her hand go to better navigate through the heavy traffic. They rode the rest of the way in silence, each sharing a quiet smile with the other.

Over the next few days, through the ins and outs of everyday and not so everyday life, they would accomplish much. Lectures, seminars and a most brilliant presentation by Dr. Evelina Gateva, applauded at the Moscow University. They even had time to plan where they would go next and where to start when they returned to Sofia.

"I am not too sure I want to go back, just yet." Georgi laughed one evening after just such a conversation. "After not being able to leave for so long, I think I would like to see the rest of the world for a little while."

Chapter 19

❧

As it would happen, a little while would turn out to be a lot longer than either one of them had planned. Not that anyone was complaining, but between a dozen lectures and conferences to speak at and the weeding out the would-be imitators, they were both quite busy. In the time of their absence from the international scene, it had become possible for a lot of organizations to appear who used their name. The methodology however was so far removed from what they had created it was almost unrecognizable.

This was a problem. Without proper knowledge of what they were doing, so much damage could easily be done. Good thing for all involved that the political atmosphere had changed, allowing them to travel again. As soon as the false teachers were discovered and confronted, they set to work. Some were retrained in the methodology after a gentle explanation.

Others decided it might be best to leave it all together. Travel was made on both ends. Back and forth from one university to the next, travel was made on both sides for the common effort. Some days, they traveled abroad to meet the others, while some days the imitators came to them in Sofia. To the good, it was at least a pleasant surprise to discover that despite his fears, the forced isolation had not caused a disinterest amongst his peers. Quite the contrary in fact, despite the inactivity as soon as he entered the scientific world once more it was as if he'd never been cut off.

Seminars and lectures were attended, some which they headed, others they only listened. One after the other the invitations were piling in dozes at a time. It was now 1995. The world was changing everyday, baffling everyone with bright new ideas and technology and yet, it was nice to see some of the 'older' still held weight. It was strange to think of their work as an 'old' idea and they tried to make it so that it was never seen as such. Not a hard thing to do, all in all.

The process was ever evolving and being fine tuned to a point of perfection, to be handled with the utmost of care. A point he strained often as each new set of imitators were uncovered. Then, out of nowhere, seemingly, an invitation sprang up to a conference that could change everything. Invited to explain *why* these methods were so dangerous, not just to Superlearning and the imitators, but to the rest of the world in a public manner.

Of course they wanted to accept immediately and would have, had Evelina not said something. "Remember, you are no longer the director of your institute," she'd reminded him gently the day the letter arrived. "You now speak for the university as well as yourself." She was right, of course. Things had to be handled even more carefully than before and while politically, things had changed, the situation was still tender. So it was in academic life, unless you were at the top of the food chain, as it were. That being the case, they knew they would have to ask permission before addressing such sensitive subjects in public. Not a problem, they assumed, walking in the next day with their usual confidence only to be turned down.

The deputy rector of the university, who was responsible for the administrative questions had refused, to their shock and dismay.

Unfortunately, Professor Semov was no longer a rector and could not help them. This put them in a very uncomfortable position. If they could not address the severity of the situation, it seemed going on as they were was almost pointless. Why sit at a stale mate with the rest of the world, unable to rectify a problem that could have been fixed with a simple explanation. That meant only one thing. The next month or two was put to putting their affairs in order before handing in their resignation. What else could they do?

From there, plans were made for travel and they left, without much in the way of goodbye to anyone or anything. It seemed somewhat deflating, after finally getting back into the swing of things to just up and leave. On the other hand, completely unfettered and free to do as they please was something else altogether. In the time they had known each other, they had only traveled for business. Always on the trail of the project, here there and everywhere in the name of science. It was good. Now, they could go and do as they would, just because they wanted to. Not to say that they were giving up the work. As if that was even possible. But a small sabbatical, well... certainly there was nothing wrong with that.

First Switzerland, then Austria to visit several old friends. In the time before the arrest, experiments had been made and people seen and talked to. It was nice to see those faces again, just because. In fact, it was so nice they decided to stay a while. Later, they said, Italy would be nice and they both agreed. For now though, Austria was perfect. Perfect for living and laughing and even working again, once they both felt rested enough.

Ah, work again. The methodology was always developing and there were always new teachers to be trained from all over the world. Even if they weren't looking for something to do, something always found them in the form of teachers, students, and anyone who might need them.

Chapter 20

Viktorsberg, Austria, the Center of Desuggestology had been running strong for 4 years. Aimed at teachers and students all round the world, the center is a beating heart of life, love and respect for fellow humans worldwide. In the time since their settlement they had seen, done and been many things, for many, many people. Never before had such questions as "happiness" come up, something that now made Georgi sad as he looked at his love. His eyes took in her face, so familiar that it was, still able to delight in the beauty he saw there even though now, he saw her completely differently.

There were things now he noticed that he never had before. She looked tired. Too tired, for his liking. Her eyes were brighter than usually in the glassy way that told him she had been crying. Had she hidden it from him? Hidden her tears? Knowing her, as he did, the answer was probably yes. As a young man, he would have taken it personally and been hurt. Now, he knew better and knew she had only been thinking of him when she hid her crying because she knew it would hurt him terribly. The only thing she didn't know was just how much.

"And yet," Georgi sighed, green eyes squinting gently as he cleaned his glasses heart twisted painfully in his chest. "I feel like I should ask you, if you regret it?"

His eyes burned with fear as he looked at his beautiful Evelina where she still stood across the room. He could not, no, would not show her how he almost trembled in his chair, or how much he himself wanted to weep. Weep like he never had before in the face of the pure unadulterated terror that gripped him like nothing in his life ever had until this moment. What if he lost her? The pungent sound of Boris Christov was ignored as it wafted through the downstairs living room. Nothing seemed to puncture the film of pure panic that had wrapped itself around the doctor's aching heart at he looked at her.

"Of course I don't," she laughed. The notes of her tender voice rang through his ears like a shot, just as clear and precious to his ears at it always had been. He wondered, how much longer would he have that laugh to brighten his days? Would she really be snatched from him so soon? "I have traveled the world. I have lived through tyranny of communism and survived. I have help build something that will stand long, long after I am gone," she paused now and took in a breath. He watched he chest tremble with the weight of it as that brilliant confidence he admired so well seemed to waver just slightly.

"And I have loved you," she said finally, smiling at him with eyes that shone like glass. She didn't cry, thankfully, for if she had he doubted his ability to hold himself together. What irony was it that no matter what task he had crossed, he had met it head on with strength and grace, but now when he needed that strength the most he could not call it to mind.

She, on the other hand stood tall and strong. Seemingly. In the last quarter hour since she had come down and told him, he had seen her. First she would draw up, delicate little shoulders tight and determined. After a time however, they would slowly deflate and her eyes would glass over once again. He suspected she was keeping on a strong face for his benefit. How long had she cried and he not known? His face soured at the thought as bitter stomach acid tingled in his throat.

"It cannot be, Eve." He told her again, shaking his head once more. A cold feeling settled in his chest. What was this awful sensation looming over his heart that suggested otherwise?

"There is always a possibility of a mistake." Of course there was, and yet…something told him it was not. Oh, by all the stars he wanted to sob. It *must* be a mistake. Please, he thought to whomever might be listening. Please do not take her.

"You must not trust them. What is called cancer could be something completely different. We will go together and will see again. Any way, it will pass."

He knew it would indeed, in some way, or the other. Rising from his chair, his strong legs broke the distance between them with two, long striding steps. "Come here, to me." He sighed, embracing her with arms that nearly trembled.

They stayed like that for a long moment, each simply listening to the other's breath. She did not notice the catch in his breath, now and again or the crystal droplets that landed in her grey streaked hair. She did not see his face, crumbled into a mask of pain where he stood above her, praying silently to any who might hear. No. He would not let her see. One deep breath…two…a third…he breathed, slowly and softly until his eyes were clear once more and the lump in his throat had melted away. Not a single tear shone in the green eyes that looked down at her, gentle and warm as a spring morning. No, it could not be true. She was too young…They had not had enough time together. There was more stress in their lives lately and she simply needed a rest.

"You know," he said with a soft smile. "We should go out and have a cake in that café on the corner," The doctor pulled away, but only long enough to grab their coats and an umbrella. "Here, Let's go. Do you know Herr Bartl told me that in our café they have a new type of éclair. I would love to try them, wouldn›t you?" She laughed softly and nodded, turning to walk out the door as he followed.

Chapter 20

"Do you really think it will be alright," Evelina asked as they made their way down the dripping streets. The city seemed as sad as he felt with it›s dark swollen sky and it›s dripping eaves that cried on every passerby. There was that cold feeling in his chest again, that said ‹no› but he pushed it aside and smiled down at her. "Of course it will." Thunder crackled in the distance. The sky opened up to unleash every wailing sob he would not, could not let and as they stepped inside the door of the cafe, he felt his heart squeeze fit to burst.

"So long as we are together, it will always be alright."

Appendix

References based on the scientific publications by Dr Georgi Lozanov and Dr Evelina Gateva

Picture 32

A French language class for adults in the Soviet Union, demonstration of the methodology in front of the Soviet scholars, prof, Velvovsky and prof. Sviadosht and Dr Lozanov. The teacher is Mr Aleko Novakov, a scientific worker from the Institute of Suggestology, Sofia, Bulgaria, in the early1970s

Dr Gateva, Creating Wholeness Through Art, p. 59, 60

When we began experimental work on the use of art in suggestopedics, education in foreign languages at the Scientific Research Institute in Sofia was conducted in the so-called clinical variant of the suggestopedic method. This variant was published by G. Lozanov (1966, 1967, 1971) and later G. Lozanov, A. Novakov (1973). It was comprised of the following main stages:

1. Deciphering of the new material, accomplished with the help of translation, repetition and a full explanation of the lexical grammatical units included in the lesson. The lesson was a thematic dialogue(conversation) which contained about a hundred new lexical units and grammar. There were usually ten dialogues for each course in a given foreign language. The material in one course of 24 days, four hours per day, consisted of approximately 2000 lexical units plus the basic grammar.

2. Active session. The dialogue was read by the teacher with the so called "intonational swing", which meant the teacher read every word or phrase in a foreign language a few times or only once:

In a declarative way (heightened)
Quietly (in a knowing, significant way)
Authoritatively (in a sure way)

The translation was read in a low voice.

3. Passive session. The teacher again read the dialogue (this time artistically, as far as the dialogue allowed) to a background of music. The music was the same for all ten sessions in the course, and consisted in a combination of slow parts of works from the pre-classic music.

4. The students worked to learn the dialogue in various ways: through etudes, conversations in pairs, discourses, occasional elementary games and songs, listening and reading to texts, etc.

The great given lesson was reduced to activating a small part of it. Every other day a new dialogue was studied. In the active session the teacher read didactic dialogues with tri-step intonation, which most often led to monotony and a lack of artistry, because of an artificial manner in the reading of phrases.

In the passive session (with the same music of slow parts) an artistic reading was not realized since the music again created a kind of monotony, a state of full relaxation in the teacher as well as the students. Thus we noticed substantial methodological gaps, which were in contradiction with the theory of suggestology.

The Ideas and Method Developed by Georgi Lozanov through the Look of the Psychotherapist, Psychohygienist Ilya Zaharievich Velvovskyi USSR

(Suggestology and Suggestopedia 1/75,p. 15-19)
A translation from the Bulgarian Language

Our first meeting with Georgi Lozanov' method was in the summer of 1969 in Moscow during the Vth Soviet Congress of the neuropathologists and psychiatrists.

The group of participants in the congress (Prof. M.S. Lebedinksi, a chairperson of the Section of medical psychology and psychotherapy at the Society of neuropathologists and psychiatrists in the USSR; Prof. A. M. Sviadosht, a psychiatrist and a psychotherapist; Prof. Bassin, a psychologist and the author of this article) was invited to the foreign language institute "Maurice Thorez" where the first experimental course in French as a foreign language with the method of Dr Lozanov took place. The abovementioned group witnessed quite an unusual lesson, the fifth in the programme, led by a trained suggestopedagogue from the Sofia Institute of Suggestology. The range of vocabulary, acquired in such a short time, the ability to use the words in the live communication (which we personally were convinced at while testing a few students), the general emotional status of the group (one of the participants, who was invited to an interview with us, joked with the French pronunciation of one of the professors who addressed him) – all this could not but amaze us.

Due to the impression of what we had seen, we invited Dr Lozanov to deliver a speech at the meeting of the Harkov society of the psychotherapists, psychoprophylacticians, and psychohygienists. The report provoked great interest and was accompanied by big discussions. At this meeting the originality of Georgi Lozanov's ideas was revealed and at the same time a considerable resemblance to the positions of the Harkov Psychotherapeutic school of thought was seen. This led us to the idea of a broader cooperation. To this end, a number of experimental courses were held in Harkov, which allowed us to study the method not only from the viewpoint of the pure pedagogy as was the case in Moscow, but also the theoretical premises to be investigated by psychologists, clinicists, neuropathologists, psychiatrists, all from leading institutes and clinics.

Research Mehtodology

The research began in the light of the requirement of I.P. Pavlov-to establish if there is the substance which he called "the bread of science": "Mr Fact"...

The following tasks were set:

1. Is it possible in the course of a month 2000 words, expressions, structures of an unknown language to be acquired?

2. To tap the capacities of different age groups (to and above 40 years of age)

3. To see the level of the fatigue if any and to establish the exhaustion level (if any) in the central nerve system in the course of the working day in people, who continue with the usual rhythm of work and study.

4. To see the influence of the methodology upon people who have functional neuro dysfunctions and neurosis.

The experimental group was created from 12 volunteers (students, pedagogues, engineers) out of whom 9 were between 20 and 35 years of age; 3 between 45 and 60. There were two people with neurosis (one of the type of the neurasthenia and the other with anxiety suspiciousness and obsessions)

The lessons were scientifically controlled by a jury comprised of scientists: clinisists and pedagogues, under the guidance of the author of the article. The checking of the pedagogic results was done according to the traditional 5 point system and the medical and psychohygienic research included gathering of data on the subjective perceptions of the students, a psychological test, check of the nervous status, the phenomena of tiredness and paraclinic research.

Research Results

As far as the first question is concerned, the jury concluded that the programme was completely fulfilled. Between 2200 and 2300 words and expressions had been acquired.

As to the second question positive results were received from the students of all ages with the only difference that the students older than 45 did not get an excellent mark.

As far as the third question is concerned, it in no student was established that any fatigue had appeared, nor less capacity to work both during the course and in fulfilling their work responsibilities.

And finally, the forth question, for the students with neurosis there was an effect equal or typical for a well conducted course in psychotherapy: the headache, irritability, depression disappeared and good appetite, good sleep and self confidence appeared.

The Harkov psychologists, psychohygienists, psychotherapists and pedagogues established that such a result has not been seen in any of the existing methods so far.

In consequence, Georgi Lozanov's monumental labour, presented and defended as a PhD thesis, was studied by the renown medical psychologist, psychoneurologist and psychohygienist, honourary member of the Soviet Academy of Science, prof. V. N. Myasishtev, by the psychologist, pedagogue, academician and secretary of the Academy of Pedagogical Sciences of the Soviet Union A. V. Petrovski and other experts. His work got wide recognition and appreciation in the Soviet Union.

Here we will not discuss the suggestopedic method in its pedagogical and didactic part, but will consider Georgi Lozanov's work from the point of view of the technology and psychology of mental labour in the study process.

The psychohygienic essence of the suggestopedic process, from our point of view, lies in the fact that while acquiring the new information, it is taking into account the laws of the subconscious automatisms, of the reflex ties thus freeing the person from an unnecessary tension and overtension. Those authors who would like to diminish G. Lozanov's contribution to a mere tapping and use of the memory reserves, in our opinion, do not understand fully the nature of the work or cannot correctly appreciate it.

There are not such stimuli, nor such signals, which once in the memory would disappear from it. It is not so much about memorizing but rather about how automatically and at need to "recollect". Here we must specify that we disclaim the meaning of the word "hypermnesia" in hypnosis since there it is a function of the phase paradoxality where the weak signal becomes strong.

I will give an example from my practice: a colleague doctor came to our psychoprophilcatic maternity ward to give birth. When labour began she started swearing in the wildest Kazakh slang, a language known to the midwife who assisted. The analysis showed that the young mother, who was from a well educated family, had never known the Kazakh language. But after graduating from the medical school, she was sent to work in Kazakhstan and while pregnant, visited the exotic markets, where she was exposed to a great number of shouts and words unknown to her. Four months after that coming to Harkov, to give birth, she expressed them in the phase of sharpened "violence of the subcortex" and the negative induction of the cortex. The woman was reproducing the words she had heard at the market , unknown to her in the good status of the cortex. What is this all about? The separate single stimulus leaves a weak trace which does not come to surface, since it is isolated, i.e. statistically unreliable. The repeated engrams , in a statistically reliable quantity , can be slightly recalled. In the case with the woman giving birth, the neurodynamics, sharpened by the paradoxical phase conditions, had transformed the "statistically unreliable" tracks into verb forms.

"Charging of the memory" in the normal study process has to create real statistically reliable tracks. But in our opinion an important task in the field of the psychohygiene of mental work is to facilitate the expression of the memorized in a verbal motorics or activity. The more automatically it happens, the easier, with less fatigue it will be.

G. Lozanov's important contribution is that he had managed to create a methodology to mobilize the unconscious automatic charges in the memory and has also found ways for the "emerging" in the memory of phenomena which will be realized in kinesthetic actions as well as verbal, mimic and other behaviour.

If we can figuratively describe the process, with the usual forms of training, statistic reliability is achieved by shooting a bullet one at a time in one and the same place, i.e. with manifold repetition, studying in the form of cramming.

While Georgi Lozanov applies *(here I do not know the military term: when shooting at many targets simultaneously ??V.)* giving the same information at different intonation frequencies. And because this is done in the ambience of concert pseudopassivity, at the level of the unconscious activity of the psyche, it is that psychological effect which defines the sharp diminishing of the fatigue and increasing of the emotional comfort. In a word, only with this approach does it make sense to understand the Lozanovian notions of "directness", "quickness", "preciseness", "economy" described in his thesis as main features of the instruction process of new type, created by him.

I would like to discuss here another notion, introduced by G. Lozanov, perhaps not too precise, but full with deep sense : concert pseudopassivity. Is it hypnosis? Or hypnosuggestion?! We are in accord with G. Lozanov that this is not hypnosis. This is using the phase surrounding at the absence of *(here I do not know how to translate it: it has to do with motor and vegetative tension but the first part talks also about agitated orientation)* Besides, the phase surrounding, unlike hypnosis, is natural. In G. Lozanov's method (and we would rather say – in the system of psychohygienopedia) the music pieces, without blocking the acquiring of information, play a serious healing role.

We will underline again that not only charging the information but also its reproduction, realized in the act of behaviour comprise a serious side in the proposed system. This is achieved with the introduction of a whole array of elements in the contemporary activating and stimulating group psychotherapy. From the outside this section looks as if "polar" to the "concentrative pseudopassiveness". Here the stress is on the "infanilisation", role play, I should say, changing of the social communication of the adults, their uniting in a certain "common act". With the same mechanisms work the "ricochet psychotherapy" and the law of Behterev of imitation as well as the psychotherapeutic theatre without the false Freudian and neo-Freudian layers.

None of the Soviet scientists studying the theoretical premises of the system could not find Freudian stands here. The notion that the psyche is not single layered and there are both conscious and subconscious sides to it is precisely the rational and not mistaken part from Freud's views. I.P. Pavlov's theory has never been in opposition to this aspect. The vice in of Freudian theory is not in the recognition of the unconscious but in the idealistic, psychobiological definition of consciousness and psyche, in proclaiming the libidian, infantile drives as the Molloh of psyche.

But there is not a trace in this in the completely materialistic ideas of the reserves of the human personality, hidden in the subconscious psychic activity as given by G. Lozanov. His term "infantilisation" (in the sense of liberating the adult person from the communicative stiffness) can be only to the prejudiced and badly informed person an indication for the traces of the Freudian infantile libidian traces.

G. Lozanov is a conspicuous and steady materialist and his "suggestology" as a study of the "common connexions" has nothing to do with Freudism.

Thus those were the considerations which rose in the mind of the psychotherapist-psychohygienist while studying the method (no, once again we will say, the system) of Dr Georgi Lozanov.

Here we cannot go into reasoning about the terms of "suggestology" and "suggestopedia" – this is the realm of the hard and fast copyright laws.

G. Lozanov clearly separates suggestion from hypnosis. He unambiguously renounces the antipsychohygienic methods of hypnopedia and nictopedia. His theoretical stand about suggestology,sharply separated from the hypnosuggestion, urge us to reconsider our dichotomical classification in the psychotherapeutic methods and to build it in such a way as not to mingle the hypnotic with the suggestive. We have not specified our new classification yet but under the influence of G. Lozanov's ideas we are looking for new characteristics of the psychotherapeutic effects.

As a conclusion we would like to express our conviction that the contribution of the Bulgarian psychotherapist Georgi Lozanov and his collaborators is a contribution to humanity.

With all my gratitude to you and all my love for Dr Lozanov....

❧

Dr Lozanov's work as a doctor and researcher before the creation of the institute of suggestology

At Sri Yogendra Yoga Institue with the teacher,
his wife and son, Bombay, India
COPYRIGHT PHOTO BY F. ROBINSON, 8.03. 1967

With an Indian Yoga 8.03.1967
COPYRIGHT PHOTO BY F. ROBINSON, 8.03. 1967

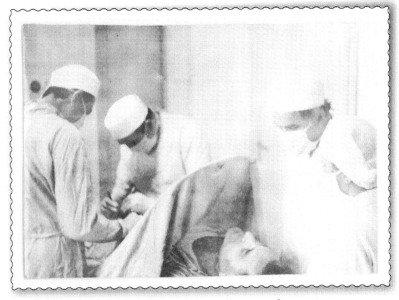

A 50 min inguinal hernia operation by means of suggestion
in a waking state. 24.08.1965, Sofia Bulgaria. The surgeons are
Dr Veselin Tanev and Dr Ivan Kalapov.

SUGGESTOLOGY

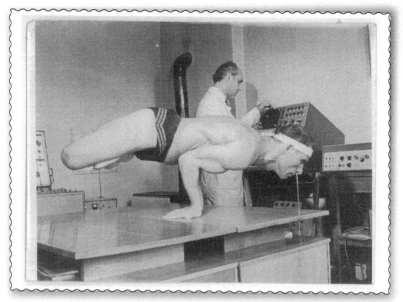

At the State Research Institute of Suggestology, Sofia, Bulgaria,
Dr Petar Balevski is measuring the brainwaves of a Bulgarian yoga

Dr Ivan Kalapov, dr Veselin Tanev have performed an operation without drug anesthesia
but via a method developed by the Bulgarian psychotherapist from
the Postgraduate Medical Institute in Sofia, Bulgaria, Dr Georgi Lozanov, 24.08.1965
(PICTURE FOR THE BTA BY B. TODOROV)

Dr Lozanov in a session of a group integral psychotherapy,
Bankia, Bulgaria

Dr Lozanov is investigating Vesa, a Bulgarian Clairvoyant

Dr Lozanov is investigating Vanga Dimitrova,
a Bulgarian Clairvoyant, Petrich, Bulgaria

Dr Lozanov is at a Conference in Moscow on parapsychology together
with the Soviet professor Naumov

Dr Lozanov is delivering his report at the International Week of Psychosomatic Medicine in Rome, 11-16 September 1967. It will be the first time the term suggestopedia is introduced as a coined word in the English language.

(Foto Sbaraglia, Roma)

School suggestopedia in Bulgaria
and Austria in the 1970s

Second grade children at an experimental school in Sofia are studying English, 1970s

Ballet in the classroom. A student at the ballet school in Sofia is dancing in the intermission between act 1 and two of a foreign language course for 2 grade students, Sofia, Bulgaria, 1970s

A second grade class at an experimental school in Sofia, Bulgaria are participating in a foreign language play: Where are Horse and Dog. The teachers are Lyubov Kozhuharova, performing, Galia Mateva and Dr Evelina Gateva (observing) (at the window)

166   SUGGESTOLOGY

On the back of the picture it is written: This is how we want all our children to be at school (The girl is a second grade student at an experimental school in Sofia, 1970s)

A live performance of a scene from the 3 opera for studying mathematics in the first grade "A World of Tales", libretto and music by Evelina Gateva. Performing artists from the State Opera Theatre in Sofia, Bulgaria, 1975.

Ballet in the classroom in the intermission of a foreign language class for second grade students in an experimental school, Sofia, Bulgaria

Dr Georgi Lozanov, April 2007, in front of the Vienna Pedagogic Academy

SUGGESTOLOGY

Dr Evelina Gateva performing in a first grade class at an experimental school, Sofia, Bulgaria, 1970s

Ballet performance in the classroom for the first grade students, an intermission in the lesson, Sofia, Bulgaria, 1970s

Language teachers from the State Research Institute of Suggestology performing the introduction lesson of "Friends", an English as a foreign language suggestopedic play for the second grade students at the experimental schools in Sofia, Bulgaria, 1970s

A lesson in Mathematics for the first grade children at an experimental school in Sofia, Bulgaria, 1970s

A first grade experimental class at the State Pedagogic Academy in Vienna, studying Mathematics with a puppet play, teacher Frau Messerer

A visit of the Bulgarian Minister of Culture Mrs Lyudmila Zhivkova and the Wife of the Iranian Scha (I think this is Farah Pahlavi) to a kindergarten of a group of 3 year old children at an experimental school in Gorna Banya, Sofia, Bulgaria, (after 1976)

Are related to the history
of the Institute of Suggestology: school suggestopedia,
teacher training and adult language courses

The State Research Institute of Suggestology, Sofia, Bulgaria, in the 1970s
(The Institute was open in 1966 and existed until 1991 as a state institution)
(Dr Lozanov had been the director of the institute from 1966 till 1984)

Dr Lozanov in his study at the Institute, the 1970s, Sofia, Bulgaria

Dr Georgi Lozanov and his team from the Institute of Suggestology together with Prof. Ilya Zaharievich Velvovsky, a Ukranian renown psychotherapist and Dr Lozanov's tutor, at the train station in Sofia (sometime between 1966 and 1972)

Dr Lozanov and Dr Gateva in Rila Mountains, mount Musala

Evelina Gateva and her adult students at an Italian course at the Institute of
Suggestology, Sofia, Bulgaria (a dance in the garden as part of the lesson), in the 70s

At the State Research Institute of Suggestology, at the Music production studio (this is the place where the concert session music was played and controlled at the appropriate moment and the sound was heard in the suggestopedic classroom), in the 70s, Sofia, Bulgaria

The first experimental 10th grade class studying all subjects suggestopedically at the State Research Institute of Suggestology, Sofia, Bulgaria, 1970

Engeneer Lakyurski is teaching algebra suggestopedically to the 10th grade
experimental class at the institute of Suggestology. EEG measure of the brainwaves of
the students, Sofia, Bulgaria, 1970

A French language class for adults in the Soviet Union, demonstration of the
methodology in front of the Soviet scholars, prof, Velvovsky and prof. Sviadosht and
Dr Lozanov. The teacher is Mr Aleko Novakov, a scientific worker from the Institute of
Suggestology, Sofia, Bulgaria, in the early1970s

An Italian language class for adults at the Institute of Suggestology, Sofia, Bulgaria. The teacher is Mrs Evelina Gateva. Sofia, Bulgaria, after 1975.

A group of Canadian teacher trainees at the Institute of Suggestology in Sofia, Bulgaria, beginning of 1970s. With Gabriel Racle.

Are all images of Dr Lozanov's international activity and simposia

Prof. Stanley Krippner, Prof. Cecilia Polack, prof. Winikamen at the UNESCO meeting on Suggestology and Suggestopedia, together with the Bulgarian minister of Education. 11-16 December 1978, Sofia, Bulgaria

Dr Lozanov with his students at a conference in memoriam to Dr Evelina Gateva
14 October 1997, Vienna, Austria

Dr Lozanov delivering a lecture at Sanno College, Tokyo, Japan, 1989

Dr Lozanov and Dr Gateva together with their close student and friend Setsuko Iki and the head of Sanno College, 1989, Tokyo, Japan

Dr Lozanov and Dr Gateva delivering a lecture at Sanno College, Tokyo, Japan, 1989 conference at the University of Athens, 1990

SUGGESTOLOGY

Dr Lozanov and Dr Gateva delivering a lecture in Florence, Italy, 1991

Dr Lozanov and Dr Gateva together with Setsuko Iki and other teachers at a seminar and teacher training in Sunny Beach, Bulgaria, 1987

At a conference in Geneve organized by Cristal Landahl, a Swedish Suggestopedagogue

Dr Lozanov and dr Gateva at a conference on Suggestology and Development
of Personality at Sofia University, Sofia, Bulgaria 1987

Dr Lozanov in Ottawa, Canada.

Dr Lozanov and Dr Gateva, together with Cristal Landahl and Greek teachers at a conference at Athens University, 1990

Dr Lozanov delivering a lecture at a conference on suggestopedia
in Viktorsberg, Austria, 1994

Dr Lozanov, Dr Gateva with the participants at the International Conference
on Suggestopedia, Saltsburg, Austria, October 26-28, 1990

Dr Lozanov and Dr Gateva with the participants at the International Conference on Suggestopedia, Salzburg, October 26-28, 1990

For more information on courses, seminars, workshops and other programs being conducted by those who are officially part of
Dr Lozanov's Foundation

please visit:

www.Suggestology.com

or

www.GeorgiLozanov.com

Made in the USA
Lexington, KY
14 February 2014